PHOTOGRAPHY BY STEPHEN BACCON

HarperCollins*Publishers*

BONDI HARVEST

GUY TURLAND
& MARK ALSTON

CONTENTS

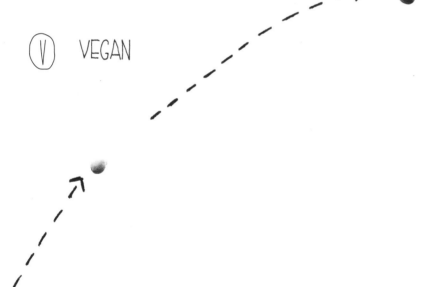

Ⓟ PALEO

Ⓥ VEGAN

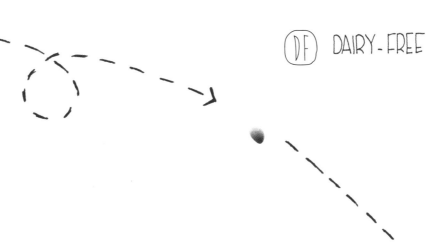

GF GLUTEN-FREE

DF DAIRY-FREE

THE BONDI HARVEST STORY

Seasonal. Sustainable. Simple. Shareable.

Bondi Harvest is a collaboration between two mates – Mark Alston and Guy Turland. Mark is a film-maker and Guy is a chef, who runs a café in North Bondi called the Depot. They started talking in November 2012, sitting on a grassy nature strip opposite the café overlooking the golden curve of Bondi Beach. Mark had been looking for a chef to work with on some cooking videos, and when he started talking to Guy and hearing his philosophy of sourcing local produce and cooking as seasonally and sustainably as possible, something clicked. They started making short cooking videos under the name Bondi Harvest and putting them up on a YouTube channel. It was guerrilla-style film-making, featuring just Guy and a camp oven, cooking whenever and wherever: on the beach, on rooftops, on boat ramps and in friends' houses. The videos were sunlit, relaxed, casual, fun – it was all about ease and flavour. The response was immediate and overwhelming. Some 18 months later, Bondi Harvest has built a passionate global fan base, with over 1 million views of their videos to date, a restaurant, and, now, a book.

We are so stoked to be writing a book that is a reflection of Bondi and the people who live here. 'Bondi' is an Aboriginal word that means 'the noise of water breaking over rocks', and it seems appropriate to first acknowledge the traditional custodians of the land. Bondi is more than just a beach – it's the beating heart of Sydney and the first stop for most overseas travellers. It's an amazing, eclectic community; a melting pot of cultures, flavours, trends, and parties. It's where travellers and backpackers, generations-old immigrants, and families with young children all live side by side. It's where morning soft-sand runners meet party people still out from the night before. It's green smoothies for breakfast and cocktails at sunset. Yoga in the morning, surfing in the afternoon and partying at dusk. From grommet surfers to orthodox Jews to old nonnas, the relatively short stretch of sand that is Bondi Beach is a unique and special community, and from that comes a unique and special lifestyle and approach to food.

This book is a celebration of this community through food.

Bondi food is light and fresh, influenced by the beach and outdoors, by fashion and trends. If it's a hot trend, it's here in Bondi. But Bondi is also where trends are started, where recipes are invented and customers are curious, hungry and looking for something new.

Guy: Nowhere else in Australia do you find such a mix of culture, food, and ocean. This unique setting has seen the emergence of some of Sydney's most important eateries and unique food offerings, each serving their version of the Bondi flavour yet united by their approach to fresh flavours and healthy offerings.

Personally my food journey began growing up with my mum who was an elite athlete. We were taught to approach food as fuel. Then when I did my apprenticeship and worked in some of the top fine dining restaurants in Australia, it was a different story. Food was a combination of flavour and art! Now living in Bondi it's the perfect mix of those two influences. Opening the Depot café gave me the freedom to run my own kitchen and develop my own style and balanced approach. I'm always asking myself, 'How can I make healthy actually bloody tasty?'

Mark: The idea of community is really important to our food, and in this book you'll find many great recipes designed to be shared with friends, families and communities. We would love nothing more than to think there could be kitchens, barbecues and parties right around the globe dishing out our Bondi-inspired food.

Bondi food is not just a flavour, it's an approach. A combination of world flavours, techniques and trends, invention, innovation, and a community looking for the next thing. A balancing act between healthy and indulgent. Set next to one of the best strips of sand in the world. What more could you want?

We hope you enjoy Bondi Harvest's recipes.

MARK

GUY

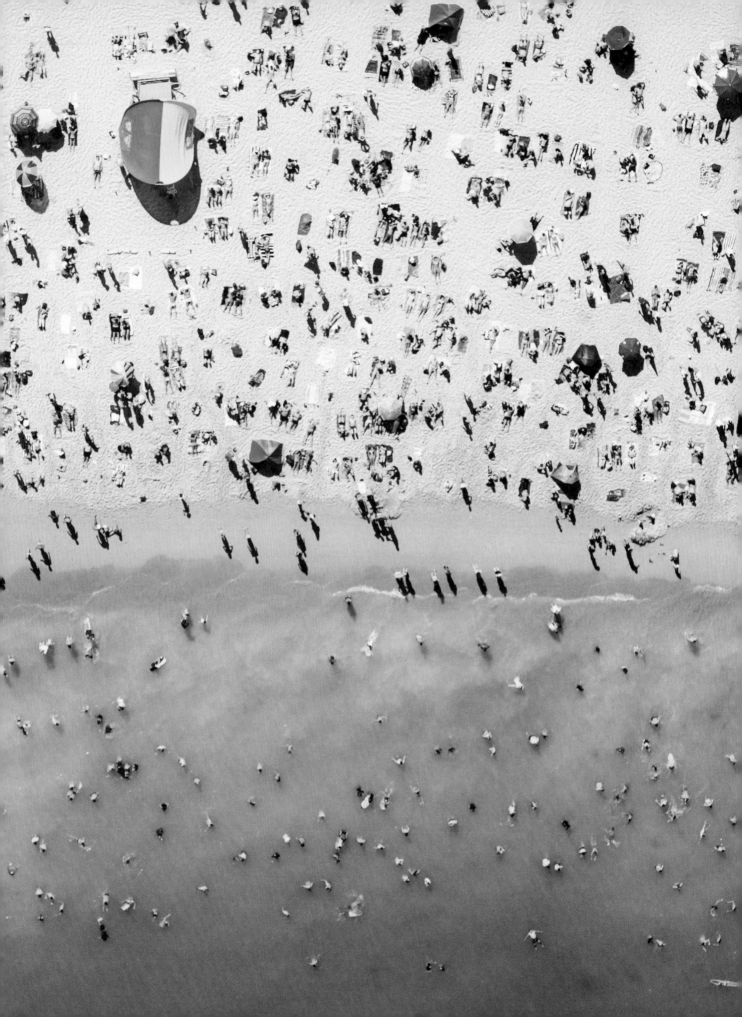

CLEAN LIVING

We reckon some people's ideas on what makes a healthy diet have become confused and twisted. For us, it's about balance. Clean living isn't some revolutionary or complicated idea – it's simply about eliminating all the crap and going back to some simple healthy-eating principles.

For starters, eat good-quality food. This means looking for whole foods, vegetables, fruits and nuts. Choose what's seasonal, fresh and organic where possible.

Secondly, don't eat too much of one thing or eliminate any of the food groups.

And remember – sometimes simple is all you need, but we all deserve to let loose every now and then.

5 TIPS FOR CLEAN LIVING

- Limit processed foods
- Eat less meat and more vegetables
- Watch your salt intake
- Eat whole grains
- Exercise regularly

BREAKFAST

Guy: Owning the Bondi Harvest restaurant and the Depot café means you get to know the locals – you see them every day and they become like your family. Our Depot café, up on the North Bondi hill, is at the heart of the local community. The doors have been open for five years now – long enough for us to have seen the local babies grow up and start school, and we've watched the bigger kids finish school and then come work in the café. This community around the Depot is what makes my day so fun.

I think you could say we are best known for our breakfast – which is an important meal here in Bondi. We love experimenting with ingredients and flavours, and getting our regulars to try interesting new dishes as well as their old favourites. The quinoa pancakes, turmeric smoothie and tri-grain brekkie bowl are all clean-living favourites at the café and restaurant.

Weekends in the summer are crazy for us, and the place is packed from the moment we open the doors at 6am right through to closing time.

But in Bondi, any time of the day, on any day, is a good time for breakfast!

COFFEE GRIND

You can't go without good coffee in Bondi, and luckily everywhere you look there's plenty on offer! But if you're in a part of the world that doesn't have coffee on every corner, or you want to make a really good cup at home, here is a simple guide to the right grind for whatever you like.

THE RIGHT GRIND	TYPE OF EQUIPMENT/COFFEE
Extra coarse grind	Cold drip
Coarse grind	French press
Medium-coarse grind	Chemex brewer
Medium grind	Drip pots
Medium-fine grind	Pour-over coffee and Aeropress
Fine Grind	Espresso and stove-top
Extra-fine grind	Turkish coffee

ULTIMATE HYDRATING ICED TEA

Hot summer days in Bondi beg for refreshing drinks like this. Load up on green tea antioxidants, hydrate with electrolyte-filled coconut water and cool off with cucumber, lime and gut-soothing aloe vera. Hot summer's night? Add a splash of gin!

> 500 ml (17 fl oz/2 cups) green tea, frozen in
>   ice-cube trays
> 12 grapes
> 1 tablespoon honey
> 1 small handful mint
> juice of 1 lime
> 300 ml (10½ fl oz) coconut water
> ½ Lebanese cucumber, sliced
> 1 tablespoon chia seeds
> 1 teaspoon aloe vera juice

Put the green tea ice cubes, grapes, honey, mint, lime juice, coconut water and cucumber in a jug, and stir.

Add the chia seeds and aloe vera and stir. Set aside for 10 minutes to allow to thicken.

IMMUNE-BOOSTING KOMBUCHA FRAPPE

Kombucha is a fermented drink full of probiotics that promotes good gut health. Make it yourself or pick up a bottle from your local health or natural food store.

> 100 ml (3½ fl oz) kombucha
> flesh and water from 1 young coconut
> 1 cm (½ inch) piece fresh ginger, peeled and
> coarsely chopped
> 1 lemon, peeled
> 1 tablespoon chia seeds
> ½ cup ice cubes
> 300 g (10½ oz) frozen pineapple
> 1 handful mint
> 2 tablespoons honey

Put all the ingredients in a blender and blend until smooth.

ANTIOXIDANT SMOOTHIE

This smoothie is epic − not just because of its vibrant colour but because it's packed full of antioxidants to get your skin glowing, your energy levels cranking and your immune system firing on all cylinders.

> 80 g (2¾ oz/½ cup) blueberries
> 200 ml (7 fl oz) coconut water
> 2 tablespoons coconut flesh
> ½ kiwifruit
> ½ lemon
> 1 tablespoon chia seeds
> ½ cup ice cubes
> 1 tablespoon goji berries
> 1 teaspoon acai powder

Put all the ingredients in a blender and blend until smooth.

CHOC SUPERFOOD SMOOTHIE

Just like a chocolate milkshake … only healthy enough to drink for breakfast. For real! This smoothie is full of superfoods like cacao, goji berries and maca, but the secret is in the avocado. If you've never had avocado in a smoothie before, prepare to have your mind blown.

> ½ avocado
> 1 tablespoon raw cacao
> 1 tablespoon raw cacao nibs
> tiny pinch of dried chilli
> 1 frozen banana
> 125 ml (4 fl oz/½ cup) coconut milk
> 4 spinach leaves
> 1 tablespoon goji berries, plus extra for garnish
> ½ teaspoon maca powder

Put all of the ingredients plus 125 ml (4 fl oz/½ cup) water in a blender and blend until smooth. Pour into a glass and garnish with extra goji berries.

ANTIOXIDANT SMOOTHIE

CHOC SUPERFOOD SMOOTHIE

IMMUNE-BOOSTING KOMBUCHA FRAPPE

DELECTABLE GREEN SMOOTHIE

DELECTABLE GREEN SMOOTHIE

Tried a green smoothie in the past you had to force down for the good of your insides? Well, this one is sweet, delicious, easy to drink and full of all the right stuff.

300 ml (10½ fl oz) coconut water
½ pear
½ avocado
10 mint leaves
¼ Lebanese cucumber
45 g (1½ oz/1 cup) baby spinach leaves
30 g (1 oz/¼ cup) vanilla protein powder
1 teaspoon goji berries
1 teaspoon activated pepitas (available from
  health or natural food stores)
1 teaspoon bee pollen (available from health
  or natural food stores)

Put the coconut water, pear, avocado, mint, cucumber, spinach leaves and protein powder in a blender and blend until smooth.

Serve in glasses, sprinkled with the goji berries, pepitas and bee pollen.

CHOC MUD BREAKFAST BOWL   Serves 1

So thick and luscious you need to serve it in a bowl and eat it with a spoon, this smoothie tastes like chocolate mousse but is healthy enough to kick-start your day. It would also make an epic quick and easy dessert when mates drop by! Yeew!

125 ml (4 fl oz/½ cup) almond milk
80 g (2¾ oz/½ cup) chia seeds
1½ frozen bananas
½ avocado
1 tablespoon raw cacao powder
2 tablespoons maple syrup or raw honey
½ teaspoon ground cinnamon
200 ml (7 fl oz) coconut water
½ cup ice
100 g (3½ oz) activated almonds (see page 226)
½ tablespoon bee pollen (available from health
  or natural food stores)
1 teaspoon toasted coconut
1 tablespoon goji berries

Put the almond milk in a jug and add the chia seeds. Stir until the mixture begins to thicken and set aside for 10 minutes.

Put the bananas, avocado, cacao, maple syrup, cinnamon, coconut water and ice in a high-speed blender and blend until smooth. Add the almond milk and chia and pulse a few times until just combined. Add a little more ice or frozen banana if you're after a thicker consistency.

To serve, spoon into a cold bowl and sprinkle over the activated almonds, bee pollen, toasted coconut and goji berries.

FRIED EGGS (GF) (P) *Makes 2*

Until you've fried eggs in coconut oil, you haven't lived. The medium chain fatty acids in coconut oil make it one of the healthiest oils on the market. Sprinkle a few chilli flakes over your eggs for an extra kick!

2 teaspoons coconut oil
2 eggs

Heat the coconut oil in a frying pan over high heat. Crack the eggs into the pan and cook for 30 seconds. Reduce the heat to low and cook until the egg white is completely cooked and no longer translucent. Season with salt and pepper.

SCRAMBLED EGGS (GF) (P) *Serves 3*

The secret to the perfect scramble lies in the cream. Along with butter, cream is a healthy saturated fat that has gotten a bad wrap for being unhealthy for far too long. Enjoy it in moderation and savour every mouthful. This scrambled egg is a perfect way to do just that.

5 eggs, lightly beaten
125 ml (4 fl oz/½ cup) cream (or almond milk if paleo)
3 teaspoons butter or coconut oil

To make the egg base, whisk the eggs and cream together in a bowl.

Pan method

Heat the butter or coconut oil in a frying pan with a heavy base or a non-stick frying pan over high heat. Add the egg mixture, reduce the heat to medium and use a spatula or wooden spoon to move the egg around gently for 5–7 minutes. Remove the pan from the heat just before it reaches the consistency you want because the egg will continue to cook a little.

Water bath method

This method takes longer but the result is silky smooth scrambled egg.

Half fill a small saucepan with water and put over medium heat, bringing the water to a simmer.

Put the egg mixture in a glass bowl and place over the saucepan to create a water bath.

Use a spatula or wooden spoon to move the egg about until it is silky smooth and cooked, or about 15 minutes. Fold through the butter or coconut oil and serve.

Making GREAT eggs is EASY to LEARN

POACHED EGGS   Makes 2

Perhaps the most popular style of egg ordered at Depot in North Bondi. Most people are terrified to give poachies a go at home, but they're super easy once you know how. The three essentials for perfect poached eggs are the ideal heat, fresh eggs and vinegar.

1 tablespoon vinegar
2 fresh eggs

Put 5 litres (10 pints/20 cups) of water in a large saucepan over high heat and bring to the boil. Reduce the heat to medium-low and when the water comes to a light simmer, add the vinegar.

Carefully crack each egg into a coffee cup or ramekin, then gently slip into the simmering water. Cook the eggs for about 4–5 minutes, then gently remove with a slotted spoon.

3 hints

The temperature is super important and can be the difference between the perfect tear-drop shaped poached eggs and a big mess. If the water is too hot, the movement and bubbling of the water will break your eggs up before they have a chance to set. If the water is not hot enough, the egg will sink to the bottom of the pan and stick to the base. The perfect water temperature for poached eggs is a light simmer at 80–83°C (175–180°F).

Adding vinegar to the poaching water not only adds an awesome zing to the poached egg but also helps the white set.

The fresher the egg the firmer the white, and a firm white will set better around and hold the yolk nicely. The white from an old egg will break down and separate itself from the yolk.

QUINOA PORRIDGE Serves 4-6

Super healthy and a great alternative to oats, this quinoa porridge is infused with warming spices and honey. It's one of our favourite ways to start a winter's day. If it's summer in your neck of the woods today, make it into a quinoa bircher (see page 36).

> *1 cinnamon stick*
> *½ vanilla bean, split and seeds scraped*
> *1 star anise*
> *1 whole clove*
> *250 g (9 oz) quinoa*
> *250 ml (9 fl oz/1 cup) coconut cream*
> *2 tablespoons honey*
> *2 tablespoons almond meal*
>
> *COMPOTE*
> *1 tablespoon chai leaves*
> *zest of 1 lemon*
> *3 dried figs*
> *3 tablespoons goji berries*
> *1 tablespoon dried cranberries*
> *1 tablespoon chia seeds*

To make the compote, put 200 ml (7 fl oz) water in a small saucepan over medium heat. Bring to a simmer and add the chai leaves and lemon zest. Simmer for 5 minutes. Strain the tea leaves and zest and discard.

Put the dried figs, goji berries, cranberries and chia seeds in a medium bowl and combine. Pour the chai tea over the mixture and set aside for at least 2 hours.

To make the porridge, put 300 ml (10½ fl oz) water in a medium saucepan over medium heat. Bring to a gentle simmer and add the cinnamon, vanilla seeds, star anise, clove and quinoa. Reduce to medium-low and simmer for 15 minutes, or until the quinoa is soft and cooked.

Add the coconut cream and continue to cook until thick and creamy. Stir through the honey and almond meal. Serve the porridge with the fruit compote.

THIS RECIPE IS JUST SO GOOD...YEW!

QUINOA BIRCHER WITH BAKED PLUMS Serves 2

Bircher is our summer version of porridge. This quinoa one is the perfect breakfast to have prepped and ready in the fridge. We like to make a big batch, scoop a serve into a jar and race out the door.

200 g (7 oz) almonds
1 cup quinoa porridge (see page 35)
260 g (9¼ oz/1 cup) natural yoghurt
2 tablespoons chia seeds

BAKED PLUMS
zest of 1 lemon
1 vanilla bean, split and seeds scraped
1 tablespoon honey
2 teaspoons coconut oil
2 plums, halved and stones removed
2 sprigs rosemary, leaves picked

Put the almonds and 300 ml (10½ fl oz) water in a container. Allow to soak overnight to activate the almonds.

To make the baked plums, preheat the oven to 175°C (345°F). Put the lemon zest, vanilla seeds, honey and coconut oil in a medium bowl and combine to form a paste. Add the plums and stir to coat in the honey paste.

Scatter the rosemary leaves over a baking tray and spoon the plum mixture on top. Bake for 15–20 minutes, or until the plums are soft.

To serve, combine the quinoa porridge base and yoghurt in a bowl. Top with the baked plums and sprinkle with the activated almonds and chia seeds.

Guy playing DRESS
ups again....HAHA

Early morning SURFS are the BEST way to start the DAY

SMOKED SALMON SOUFFLÉ

Makes 6 x 240 ml (8 oz) ramekins

The ultimate show-off breakfast! Soufflé is one of those dishes many people avoid making, but it's not as tricky as you might think and über impressive to serve friends for Sunday brekkie!

> 100 g (3½ oz) butter
> 200 g (7 oz/1⅓ cups) plain (all-purpose) flour
> 250 ml (9 fl oz/1 cup) thin (pouring) cream
> 100 g (3½ oz) parmesan cheese, grated, plus extra
>   for sprinkling
> 2 teaspoons dijon mustard
> 4 egg yolks
> 1 large handful parsley, finely chopped
> 1 handful dill, finely chopped
> zest of 1 lemon
> 200 g (7 oz) smoked salmon, flaked
> 6 egg whites

Preheat the oven to 175°C (345°F).

Melt half the butter in a medium saucepan over medium heat. Sift the flour into the saucepan over the melted butter and mix until smooth. Cook for 1 minute, not allowing the mixture to colour. Add the cream slowly and cook, mixing constantly, for 2–3 minutes, or until smooth and thick. Stir in half the parmesan cheese and all of the mustard.

Transfer one-third of the cheese mixture to a medium bowl. Add the egg yolks and stir to combine, then return this mixture to the saucepan and cook for 30 seconds. Set aside to cool to room temperature.

Add the parsley, dill, lemon zest and smoked salmon to the saucepan and mix gently to combine.

Grease the inside of the ramekins with the remaining butter. Dust with a little parmesan cheese.

In a clean medium bowl, whisk the egg whites until firm peaks form.

Very gently, trying not to beat out any of the air, fold one-third of the egg white into the cheese mixture to lighten it. Once combined and smooth, add the remaining egg white and fold in gently.

Pour the mixture into the prepared ramekins. Sprinkle over the remaining parmesan cheese, and grind over salt and pepper, then run your finger around the rim of the ramekin (this will help the soufflé rise evenly).

Bake for 20–30 minutes and serve immediately.

KALE SHAKSHUKA Serves 4-6

We love making this shakshuka in one big pan and serving it on the table for people to help themselves. But you can prepare it in individual ramekins – put the tomato mixture into the ramekins and crack an egg or two on top, then bake in a 180°C (350°F) oven for 10 minutes or until the egg is cooked.

> *20 ml (½ fl oz/1 tablespoon) olive oil*
> *1 onion, finely diced*
> *2 garlic cloves, crushed*
> *1 red capsicum (pepper), finely diced*
> *2 long red chillies, finely diced*
> *2 tablespoons tomato paste (concentrated purée)*
> *1 teaspoon sweet paprika*
> *1 teaspoon smoky paprika*
> *1 teaspoon ground cumin*
> *425 g (1 lb) tin diced or crushed tomatoes*
> *½ teaspoon brown sugar*
> *500 g (about ½ a bunch) kale, stalks removed and finely sliced*
> *6 eggs*
> *1 small handful parsley sprigs*
> *fresh crusty bread, to serve*

Heat the oil in a medium heavy-based frying pan over medium-high heat. Add the onion, garlic, capsicum and chilli. Cook for 3–5 minutes, or until tender and slightly caramelised. Add the tomato paste, paprika and cumin and cook for 1 minute, or until fragrant. Add the tomato and sugar, and stir to combine. Reduce the heat to medium-low and cook for 15–20 minutes.

Add the kale and stir through the tomato sauce. Crack the eggs one by one into the tomato mixture in the pan. Reduce the heat to low and cook for 5 minutes, or until the eggs are cooked the way you like. Scatter over the parsley, season with salt and pepper, and serve with fresh crusty bread.

QUINOA PANCAKES WITH SMOKED TROUT

Full of protein and good fats but gluten-free and dairy-free, these savoury pancakes are delicious. We've served them with a smoked trout and rocket salad, and you can throw a poached egg on top too, if you like. It would also go really well with some kale pesto (page 234) on the side. If you're looking for something sweet, replace the seasoning with a tablespoon of honey and top with yoghurt and fresh berries.

> 2½ cups cooked quinoa (see page 240)
> 130 g (4½ oz/1 cup) buckwheat flour
> 2 teaspoons baking powder
> 5 eggs
> 250 ml (9 fl oz/1 cup) coconut cream
> 50 ml (1½ fl oz/2½ tablespoons) coconut water
> coconut oil or butter, for cooking
> 300 g (10½ oz) rocket (arugula), to serve
> 200 g (7 oz) smoked trout, to serve
> poached eggs, to serve
> chia seeds, for sprinkling

To make the pancakes, put the quinoa, flour, baking powder, eggs, coconut cream and coconut water in a food processor and process for 5 minutes, or until smooth. Season with salt and pepper, transfer to a large jug or bowl.

Melt a teaspoon of coconut oil or butter in a non-stick frying pan over medium-high heat. Add ¼ cup of the pancake mixture and cook until bubbles begin to form and the edge of the pancake starts to colour. Carefully flip. Cook until golden brown, keep warm and repeat with the remaining mixture.

Put the rocket and smoked trout in a bowl and toss gently to combine. To serve, put the pancakes on the plate with the rocket and trout salad and the poached eggs sprinkled with chia seeds.

BUTTERMILK PANCAKES WITH HONEY & GINGER CARAMELISED BANANAS

 Serves 6

If you're looking for the perfect guilt-free pancake recipe, you've just struck pancake gold. These make the perfect healthy start to a lazy Sunday. You're welcome!

130 g (4½ oz/1 cup) buckwheat flour
100 g (3½ oz/1 cup) almond meal
1½ teaspoons baking powder
1½ teaspoons bicarbonate of soda (baking soda)
3 tablespoons sugar
1 egg, lightly beaten
600 ml (20 fl oz) buttermilk (see page 228)
2 drops vanilla essence
1 tablespoon coconut oil, for cooking
Greek-style yoghurt, to serve

HONEY & GINGER CARAMELISED BANANAS
1 tablespoon honey
1 cm (½ in) piece fresh ginger, finely grated
1 banana, sliced into discs
juice of 1 lemon
1 tablespoon sesame seeds

To make the honey & ginger caramelised bananas, put the honey in a small saucepan over medium heat. Cook until it begins to bubble. Add the ginger and cook for 10 minutes, or until the honey changes colour and begins to caramelise.

Add the banana to the saucepan and toss to coat in the honey mixture. Remove from the heat. Add the juice and sesame seeds, stir and set aside.

To make the pancakes, sift the flour, almond meal, baking powder, bicarbonate of soda and sugar into a large bowl.

In a separate bowl, add the egg, buttermilk and vanilla and mix until combined.

Pour the wet mixture into the dry mixture, stirring until it's a smooth batter.

Heat the coconut oil in a large frying pan over medium-high heat. Add a ¼ cup of batter per pancake. When the mixture begins to bubble, flip it and cook the other side until golden. Repeat with remaining batter.

Serve the pancakes with the honey & ginger caramelised bananas and a dollop of yoghurt.

CHOC & RASPBERRY BREAKFAST MUFFINS

 Serves 6

We worked hard on making these the moistest, tastiest, can't-believe-there's-no-gluten-in-them muffins you've ever tasted. And I think we succeeded. You be the judge.

350 g (12 oz/3½ cups) almond meal
3 teaspoons raw cacao powder
2 teaspoons baking powder
4 eggs, lightly beaten
150 ml (5 fl oz) coconut oil, melted
200 g (7 oz) honey
250 g (9 oz/2 cups) raspberries
100 g (3½ oz) young coconut flesh (scraped
  from a halved young coconut)
100 g (3½ oz) activated almonds (see page 226), plus
  12 extra for topping
160 g (5½ oz/1 cup) pitted dates

Preheat the oven to 170°C (325°F). Grease and line a 6-hole giant (Texas/1 cup) muffin tin.

When making muffins, I approach it as three mixtures — dry, wet and flavour — in three different bowls that get mixed together in the end.

Dry mixture: Combine the almond meal, cacao powder and baking powder.

Wet mixture: Combine the eggs, coconut oil and honey.

Flavour mixture: Combine 200 g (7 oz) of the raspberries and the coconut flesh, almonds and dates.

Now, fold the wet mixture into the dry mixture, then add the flavour mixture and mix gently until just combined. Spoon into the muffin tins. Combine the remaining raspberries and extra almonds and scatter over the mixture in the muffin tins.

Bake for 30–35 minutes, or until a skewer inserted into the centre comes out clean.

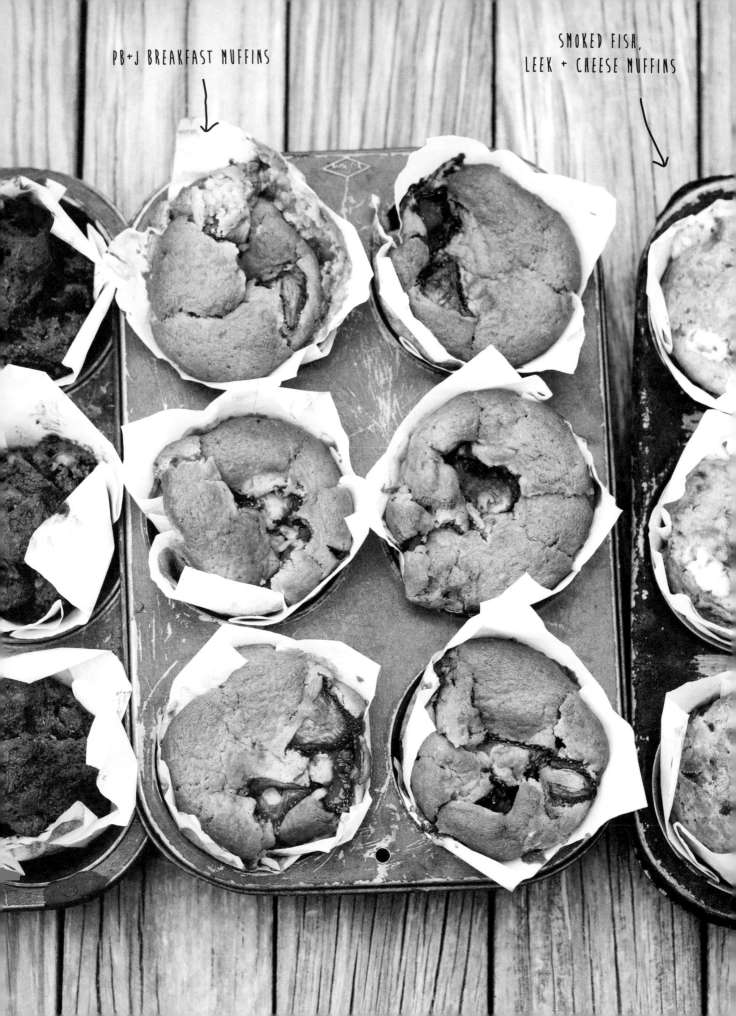

PB+J BREAKFAST MUFFINS

SMOKED FISH,
LEEK + CHEESE MUFFINS

PB+J BREAKFAST MUFFINS

SMOKED FISH,
LEEK + CHEESE MUFFINS

PB&J BREAKFAST MUFFINS   *Serves 6*

*A spin-off from the classic peanut butter and jelly sandwich –
an all-time favourite flavour combination of American youth.*

> 300 g (10½ oz/2 cups) self-raising flour
> 1 teaspoon baking powder
> 110 g (3¾ oz/½ cup firmly packed) brown sugar
> 110 g (3¾ oz/½ cup) caster sugar
> 1 egg
> 225 g (8 oz) natural yoghurt
> 160 ml (5¼ fl oz) thin (pouring) cream
> 80 g (2¾ oz) butter, melted
> 250 g (9 oz/2 cups) raspberries
> 300 g (10½ oz/2 cups) sliced strawberries
> 1 tablespoon honey
> 1 vanilla bean, split and seeds scraped
> zest of 1 lemon
> 100 g (3½ oz) homemade peanut butter (see page
>   228, 'Raw nut butter')
> 35 g (1¼ oz/¼ cup) roasted peanuts

Preheat the oven to 170°C (325°F). Grease and line a 6-hole giant
(Texas/1 cup) muffin tin.

When making muffins, I approach it as three mixtures – dry, wet and
flavour – in three different bowls that get mixed together in the end.

Dry mixture: Combine the flour, baking powder and sugars.

Wet mixture: Combine the egg, yoghurt, cream and butter.

Flavour mixture: Combine the raspberries, strawberries, honey, vanilla and
zest and let sit for 30 minutes at room temperature.

Now, fold the wet mixture into the dry mixture, then add the flavour
mixture and mix gently until just combined. Spoon into the muffin tin,
filling to halfway. Put 1 tablespoon of the peanut butter into the middle of
each muffin. Top with the remaining muffin mixture and scatter over the
roasted peanuts.

Bake for 35–40 minutes, or until a skewer inserted into the centre comes
out clean.

SMOKED FISH, LEEK & CHEESE MUFFINS   Serves 6

Who said muffins had to be sweet? The flavours in these savoury muffins will blow your mind. Make a batch and freeze them for breakfast or a snack on the go. They make perfect pre-surf fuel.

300 g (10½ oz/2 cups) self-raising flour
1½ teaspoons baking powder
50 g (1¾ oz/½ cup) grated parmesan cheese
150 g (5½ oz) hot smoked fish, flaked
1 egg, lightly beaten
225 g (8 oz) Greek-style yoghurt
160 ml (5¼ fl oz) milk
80 g (2¾ oz) butter, melted
1 tablespoon olive oil
1 leek, white part only, finely sliced
1 garlic clove, finely chopped
1 small red chilli, seeded and finely chopped
2 sprigs thyme, leaves picked
100 g (3½ oz) goat's cheese, crumbled
zest of 1 lemon
1 small handful parsley, finely chopped

Preheat oven to 170°C (325°F). Grease and line a 6-hole giant (Texas/1 cup) muffin tin.

When making muffins, I approach it as three mixtures – dry, wet and flavour – in three different bowls that get mixed together in the end.

Dry mixture: Combine the flour, baking powder, parmesan cheese and smoked fish.

Wet mixture: Combine the egg, yoghurt, milk and butter.

Flavour mixture: Heat the oil in a frying pan over medium-high heat. Cook the leek, garlic, chilli and thyme for 5 minutes, or until the leek is tender. Remove from the heat and allow to cool slightly.

Now, fold the wet mixture into the dry mixture, then add the flavour mixture and mix gently until just combined. Spoon into the muffin tin. Combine the goat's cheese, lemon zest and parsley and scatter over the mixture in the muffin tin.

Bake for 35–40 minutes, or until a skewer inserted into the centre comes out clean.

BONDI HARVEST

ME & MUM

DATE & GRANOLA BREAKFAST BAR

 Makes 10 bars

Store-bought ones are full of cr*p but these breakfast bars are effortless to make and are full of healthy, keep-you-full-all-morning ingredients. Store them in an airtight container and they'll last about a month.

> *320 g (11¼ oz/2 cups) pitted dates (I like Medjool)*
> *250 ml (9 fl oz/1 cup) coconut oil*
> *1 cm (½ inch) piece fresh ginger, coarsely chopped*
> *zest of 1 lemon*
> *4 cups Bondi Harvest granola (see page 240)*

Grease and line a 33 cm x 23 cm x 5 cm (13 inch x 9 inch x 2 inch) baking tin with greaseproof or non-stick baking paper.

Put the dates, coconut oil, ginger and zest in a food processor and process to a smooth paste.

Transfer to a large bowl and fold through the granola.

Put the mixture into the prepared tin, spread it over evenly and press into the base and side. Transfer to the fridge and allow to set. Cut into 10 bars and store in an airtight container.

DATES

ALMONDS

PEPITAS

COCO OIL

PUFFED RICE

GOJI BERRIES

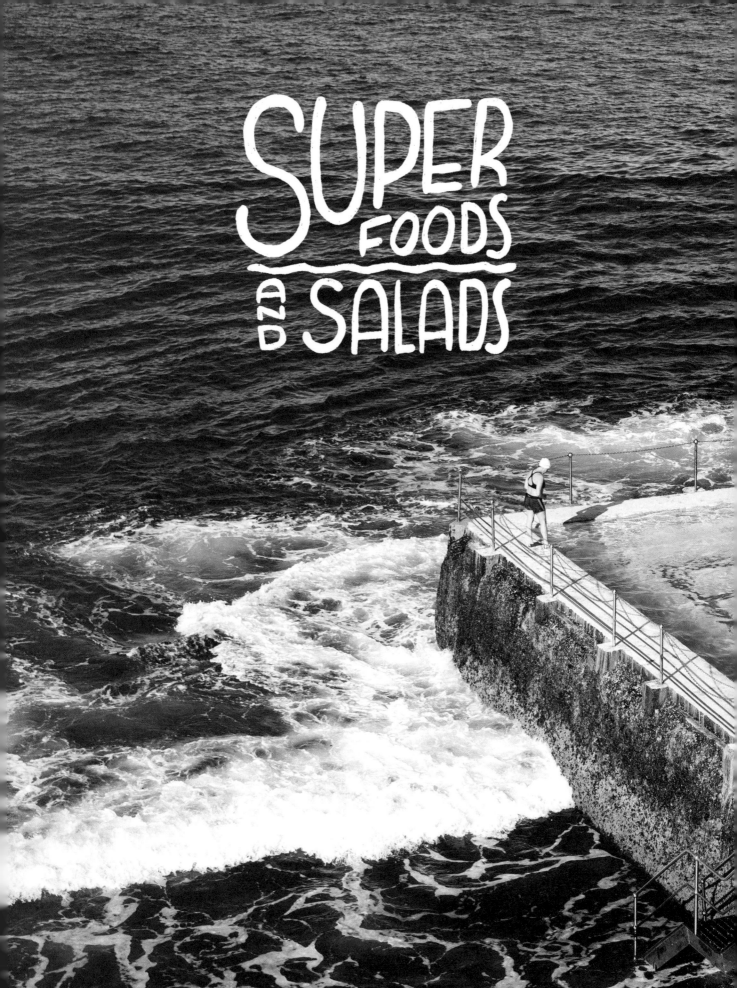

SUPER FOODS and SALADS

At Bondi Harvest we love to harvest, pick, gather and forage from our local environment.

There is nothing better than finding the perfect patch of wild seasonal greens growing along the coastline, or getting the call from a buddy to come and grab a bucket of fruit straight from the tree.

From bundles of wild lemon myrtle or fragrant bay leaf, to summer stone fruit or greens from the vegie patch, there is nothing like harvesting your own produce. And even here in Bondi there's plenty of amazing fresh food on offer – you just have to know where to look, or make the right friends!

We don't like to waste anything, so when lemons are in season, for instance, we'll grab a bunch of mates for a day of picking and make up jars of preserved lemon. Or when stone fruit is ripe, we make jam or even blend the fruit and seal it in a bag and put it in the freezer, ready for a smoothie whenever.

SUPERFOODS & SALADS PHILOSOPHY

There is no doubt that vegetables, fruits, grains and all things plant-based are having a resurgence. Whether you are trying to limit your environmental footprint by eating less meat, looking for a more paleo-style diet or interested in going completely vegetarian, there is no better time to be eating meatless.

The fact is we don't need to eat meat every day, and some of our favourite dishes are vegetarian. The colours, textures and flavours you can create using vegetables, nuts and grains is endless, and in Australia we are so lucky to have a wide array of ingredients to use and a diverse spectrum of food cultures to draw inspiration from.

It's really important to note that we created these dishes from a flavour perspective – as we always do – and to stand alone as delicious, nurturing meals. Not having meat as an ingredient doesn't make these dishes any less fulfilling – in fact the opposite is true.

At the Depot and Bondi Harvest Bondi Junction (BHBJ) we use lots of ingredients I guess you would call superfoods – kale, quinoa, blueberries and chia seeds – and they feature in many of the recipes in this book, too, because they are so good to eat regularly to increase your health and wellbeing. And these recipes show you how to make superfoods super tasty as well.

We think an important part of bringing good balance to your diet is embracing fresh produce and learning to be creative with it.

TOASTED MANGO, GINGER & CHIA SEED ROLL-UPS

Makes 10 roll-ups

This recipe takes me back to the school yard, when I would always have a roll-up or fruit leather in my lunchbox. I loved them so much, I refused to 'grow up' and stop eating them.

> *900 g (2 lb/3 cups) ripe mango, chopped*
> *1 teaspoon minced fresh ginger*
> *1 tablespoon chia seeds*
> *35 g (1¼ oz/½ cup) shredded coconut*

Preheat the oven to 150°C (300°F). Line a baking tray with baking paper.

Put the mango, ginger and chia seeds in a food processor and process until smooth.

Using an offset spatula, spread out the mango mixture evenly over the tray, about 3 mm (⅛ inch) thick. Sprinkle with the coconut and cook for 5 hours, or until the sheet is dry and pliable.

Slide the baking paper with the sheet onto a chopping board. Slice into long strips and roll up. Store in an airtight container in the fridge for up to 1 week.

HONEY COCONUT CHIPS Makes 1 tray

At BHBJ, we use the juice of thousands of drinking coconuts in smoothies, juices and frappes. I don't like wasting food so I've created a fun, healthy way to use the flesh.

> **9 coconuts (you'll need the flesh)**
> **1 tablespoon honey**

Preheat the oven to 175°C (345°F). Line a baking tray with baking paper.

Remove the juice from the coconut and reserve it for drinking or smoothies. Use a mallet to crack the coconut in half and scrape out the flesh with a spoon.

Put the coconut flesh and honey in a food processor and process until a smooth paste forms.

Using an offset spatula, spread out the coconut mixture evenly over the tray, about 3 mm (⅛ inch) thick. Cook for 4–5 hours, or until the sheet is dry to the touch. Set aside to cool for 20 minutes.

Break the coconut sheet into chips and store in an airtight container in a cool dry place for up to 2 weeks.

VANILLA HONEY CHIA CHIPS Serves 2

These chips not only look and taste epic, but they are also guaranteed to give you an energy hit. If there's any uncooked mix left over, eat it for breakfast as chia pudding.

> **½ tablespoon honey**
> **1 drop vanilla essence**
> **35 g (1½ oz/¼ cup) chia seeds**

Preheat the oven to 100°C (200°F).

Put the honey, vanilla, 250 ml (9 fl oz/1 cup) water and the chia seeds in a container with a lid. Stir, put on the lid and put in the fridge overnight to create a chia seed pudding.

Next day, line a baking tray with baking paper or use a silicone non-stick baking mat. Using an offset spatula, spread out the chia pudding evenly over the tray to a thin layer.

Bake for 30 minutes, or until the chia layer is dehydrated and crispy.

Remove from the oven to cool, break up the crispy chia layer and store in an airtight container in a dry place for up to 1 week.

BEETROOT CHIPS

  Serves 2

Prepare to be blown away by these earthy, sweet and salty flavour bombs – you'll want to keep them all to yourself.

> **3 beetroot**
> **100 ml (3½ fl oz) olive oil or coconut oil**
> **3 sprigs rosemary, leaves picked**

Preheat the oven to 150°C (300°F). Line a baking tray with baking paper.

Using a mandolin or a sharp knife, slice the beetroot into super thin slices. Place the beetroot slices in a bowl and toss with oil and rosemary. Season with salt and pepper.

Place the beetroot slices on the baking tray without any slices overlapping. Bake for 30–50 minutes, or until the beetroot is crispy.

Allow to cool to room temperature, then store in an airtight container. Keep in a cool dry place for up to 1 week.

SUPERFOOD KALE CHIPS   Serves 2

A healthy alternative to potato chips when you're looking for a savoury snack, these kale chips also make a great crunchy addition to salads and vegie dishes.

> **100 ml (3½ fl oz) coconut oil**
> **1 teaspoon sea salt**
> **1 teaspoon freshly ground black pepper**
> **zest of 1 lemon**
> **½ teaspoon paprika**
> **1 teaspoon chia seeds**
> **1 teaspoon fresh thyme leaves**
> **1 bunch kale, stalks removed**

Preheat the oven to 175°C (345°F).

Put the coconut oil, salt, pepper, lemon zest, paprika, chia seeds and thyme in a large bowl and mix to combine. Add the kale leaves and toss to coat.

Put the seasoned kale leaves on a baking tray and cook for 8 minutes, or until crispy.

Set aside to cool and store in an airtight container in a dry place for up to 1 week.

BUCKWHEAT-STUFFED CAPSICUM   Serves 4

Gone are the days of boring vegetarian options; this is one dish I'd eat over steak or grilled chicken any day. When you chargrill capsicums, it creates the most intense flavour. The heat draws out the natural sugars, caramelising the skin and leaving a tender, sweet and smoky flesh. All you need to do is cut it in half, stuff it and you've got a winning combination.

2 capsicums (peppers)
150 ml (5 fl oz) olive oil
½ onion, chopped
2 garlic cloves, minced
1 red chilli, minced
½ cup diced tomato
3 tablespoons pomegranate seeds
1 cup cooked buckwheat
1 large handful parsley, chopped, plus extra for garnish
zest and juice of 1 lemon
130 g (4½ oz/½ cup) ricotta
2 tablespoons sultanas or currants
1 small handful dill, chopped
1 small handful coriander, chopped

TAHINI DRESSING
270 g (9½ oz/1 cup) tahini (see page 228)
½ tablespoon smoked paprika
1 garlic clove, minced
½ red chilli, minced (keep the seeds if you like it hot)
zest of 1 lemon

To make the tahini dressing, put the tahini, paprika, garlic, chilli and lemon zest in a bowl or glass jar with a lid. Season with salt and pepper and whisk or shake until well combined. Set aside.

Preheat the oven to 180°C (350°F). Line a baking tray with baking paper.

Blacken the skin of the capsicums over an open flame (on a gas ring or using a blow torch) on all sides. This should take about 10 minutes and will create a sweet smoky flavour. Set aside to cool.

Cut the capsicums in half and remove the seeds and membranes. Put them on the baking tray.

To make the stuffing, heat the olive oil in a medium saucepan over medium heat. Add the onion, garlic and chilli and cook for 5 minutes, or until the onion is tender. Add the tomato and cook for 4 minutes. Transfer the mixture to a large bowl and add the pomegranate seeds, buckwheat, parsley, lemon zest and juice, ricotta and sultanas. Combine well and season with salt and pepper.

Fill the capsicum halves with the stuffing mixture and cook in the oven for 10 minutes, or until tender. Serve with the tahini dressing and scatter over the fresh herbs.

QUINOA, PUMPKIN, FENNEL & SALSA VERDE SALAD

Makes 1 large bowl

I like to use quinoa as a flavour vessel as it absorbs flavours so well. It's one of my favourite ways, along with using fresh herbs from the backyard, to bring life to a simple salad.

150 g (5½ oz/1 cup) pumpkin, chopped
150 g (5½ oz/1 cup) fennel, chopped
4 sprigs thyme
1 tablespoon fennel seeds
1 tablespoon ground cumin
150 ml (5 fl oz) vegetable oil
½ cup quinoa
250 ml (8 fl oz/1 cup) water or stock
1 sprig rosemary (optional)
1 bay leaf (optional)
1 whole garlic clove (optional)

SALSA VERDE
1 cup parsley leaves, finely chopped
1½ cups basil leaves, finely chopped
½ cup oregano leaves, finely chopped
1 garlic clove, minced
3 tablespoons capers, drained and finely chopped
1 red chilli, minced (keep the seeds if you like it hot)
150 ml (5 fl oz) olive oil
juice of 2 lemons, plus lemon wedges to serve

To cook the pumpkin and fennel, preheat the oven to 200°C (400°F). Line a baking tray with baking paper.

Put the pumpkin and fennel in a large bowl with the thyme, fennel seeds, cumin and oil. Season with salt and pepper and toss to coat the vegetables.

Put the pumpkin and fennel in one layer on the tray without any pieces overlapping. Cook for 20–30 minutes, until the vegetables are tender and caramelised. Remove from the oven and set aside to cool.

To make the salsa verde, combine the parsley, basil, oregano, garlic, capers and chilli in a medium bowl. Add the olive oil and lemon juice, mix well and set aside.

To cook the quinoa, first rinse under water in a strainer for 5 minutes. Heat the water or stock in a medium saucepan over medium heat. Add the quinoa, rosemary, bay leaf and garlic, if using. Cover and bring to the boil. Turn heat to low and cook for 15 minutes, or until the quinoa becomes translucent. Remove the garlic. While it is still warm, add the salsa verde, season with salt and pepper, and mix through.

To make the salad, put the quinoa and vegetables in a large bowl and toss to combine.

Serve in a bowl or on a platter with lemon wedges.

WARM CHICKPEA & KALE SALAD Serves 2-3

Adding chickpeas is the perfect way to turn a side salad into something more substantial for the dinner table, and warming them makes them deliciously soft and buttery.

1 tablespoon olive oil
1 garlic clove, finely sliced
½ onion, coarsely chopped
1 red chilli, finely sliced (keep the seeds if you like it hot)
1 zucchini (courgette), coarsely chopped
zest and juice of 1 orange
2 sprigs thyme
250 g (9 oz) cherry tomatoes
180 g (6 oz/1 cup) cooked chickpeas
2 large kale leaves, finely sliced

Heat the oil in a medium frying pan over medium-high heat. Add the garlic, onion, chilli, zucchini, zest and thyme and cook for 3–5 minutes, stirring, or until the onion is softened but not coloured. Season with salt and pepper, and add the tomatoes and chickpeas. Cook, stirring, for 3–5 minutes, or until the chickpeas are warmed through. Add the orange juice, mix through, and remove from the heat.

Put the kale in a large bowl and pour over the chickpea mixture while still hot. Toss well to coat and wilt the kale. Serve warm.

MELON, BASIL & FETA SALAD WITH BALSAMIC RED WINE REDUCTION

Serves 2-3

Fresh, crisp, sweet and salty, this is my go-to summer salad. Using in-season fruit in salads always makes for a refreshing change.

3 tablespoons pistachio kernels
3 tablespoons almonds
finely grated zest and juice of 4 limes
200 ml (7 fl oz) olive oil
½ cup cherry tomatoes, halved
¼ (about 250 g/9 oz) rockmelon (canteloupe),
  cut into 1 cm (½ inch) cubes
¼ (about 250 g/9 oz) watermelon, cut into 1 cm
  (½ inch) cubes
200 g (7 oz) prosciutto or smoked fish (optional),
  torn into bite-size pieces
200 g (7 oz) marinated feta cheese
1 large handful basil, leaves picked

BALSAMIC REDUCTION
1 litre (35 fl oz/4 cups) balsamic vinegar
125 ml (4 fl oz/½ cup) Marsala
125 ml (4 fl oz/½ cup) red wine

To make the balsamic reduction, put the balsamic, Marsala and red wine in a heavy-based saucepan over medium-low heat. Cook until reduced by two-thirds and thickened to the consistency of honey (this will take 2–3 hours). Remove from the heat and set aside.

Put the pistachios and almonds in a small frying pan over medium heat. Cook for 5 minutes, stirring continuously, until lightly brown. Transfer the nuts to a large bowl and allow to cool.

Put the lime zest and juice in a small bowl and add the olive oil. Whisk well using a fork or whisk.

Put the tomatoes, rockmelon and watermelon in a large bowl. Pour over the lime vinaigrette and toss lightly.

Arrange the prosciutto or smoked fish (if using) over the top, crumble over the feta, and drizzle with the balsamic reduction. Season with sea salt and freshly ground black pepper and garnish with the toasted nuts and basil leaves.

WILD RICE, PICKLED ZUCCHINI, DUKKAH & MOZZARELLA SALAD

There are so many different grains and rices out there; don't be afraid to try something new. Wild rice is fast becoming one of my favourites – just cook it like any other rice, and it develops a super tasty earthy and nutty flavour, and adds a cool texture to salads.

150 g (5½ oz/1 cup) cooked wild rice
1 large handful mint, leaves picked
300 g (10½ oz) mozzarella

QUICK PICKLED ZUCCHINI
150 ml (5 fl oz) white wine vinegar
2 tablespoons honey
½ red chilli, minced (keep the seeds if you like it hot)
2 whole cloves
1 cinnamon stick
2 cups diced (2 cm/¾ in) zucchini (courgette)

DUKKAH BREADCRUMBS
130 g (4½ oz/1 cup) hazelnuts, finely chopped
100 g (3½ oz/⅔ cup) sesame seeds
1 tablespoon coriander seeds
1 tablespoon ground cumin
zest of 1 lemon
2 teaspoons freshly ground black pepper
1 teaspoon sea salt
300 ml (10½ fl oz) olive oil
½ loaf old bread, cut into 3 cm (1¼ inch) cubes

To make the quick pickled zucchini, put the white wine vinegar in a medium saucepan over medium heat. Add the honey, chilli, cloves and cinnamon stick and bring to a simmer. Allow to simmer for 5 minutes, then remove the saucepan from the heat and add the zucchini. Set aside to infuse.

Meanwhile, make the dukkah breadcrumbs. Preheat the oven to 180°C (350°F).

Put the hazelnuts, sesame seeds, coriander seeds, cumin, lemon zest, pepper and salt in a small bowl and mix to combine. This is your dukkah mixture. Scoop 5 tablespoons of it into a large bowl, add the olive oil and mix well. (Put any remaining dukkah mixture in an airtight container to use as a garnish and for later.)

Add the bread to the large bowl and toss it with your hands until well coated with the dukkah and oil mixture. Scatter the bread over a baking tray and cook for 15–20 minutes, until golden, moving the bread around every 5 minutes to prevent it burning. Set aside to cool slightly.

To make the salad, strain the pickled zucchini and transfer to a large bowl with the wild rice, dukkah breadcrumbs and mint. Toss to combine and transfer to a serving bowl. Tear the mozzarella with your fingers and scatter over the salad. Garnish with a sprinkle of the remaining dukkah and serve.

CHILLI, LIME & GINGER BROCCOLI SALAD

   Serves 4

For those who aren't fans of broccoli – I get it, I do. But give me a chance to change your mind. It may be humble, but broccoli's a superfood that just needs a little love (and some good PR). And that's exactly what I've given it in this recipe.

1 head broccoli, broken into florets
1 yellow zucchini (courgette), finely sliced
1 avocado, cut into 1 cm (½ inch) dice
sprouted chia seeds, for sprinkling
1 small handful almonds
1 small handful coriander, leaves picked

DRESSING
150 ml (5 fl oz) coconut oil
2 teaspoons minced fresh ginger
1 teaspoon minced garlic
1 red chilli, minced
1 tablespoon sesame seeds
2 teaspoons soy sauce
zest and juice of 1 orange
zest and juice of 3 limes

Bring a large saucepan of water to the boil.

Meanwhile, to make the dressing, heat the coconut oil in a frying pan over medium heat. Add the ginger, garlic, chilli and sesame seeds and cook for 5–6 minutes, or until tender. Remove from the heat and add the soy, and the orange and lime zest and juice. Mix and transfer to a large bowl.

Add the broccoli to the saucepan of boiling water and cook for 4–5 minutes, until tender but still with some crunch. Strain and transfer the warm broccoli to the bowl with the dressing and give it a mix. (The warm broccoli will suck in all those epic dressing flavours.)

When you are ready to serve, add the zucchini and avocado, season with sea salt and freshly ground black pepper and toss lightly. Transfer to a serving bowl and sprinkle over the sprouted chia seeds, almonds and coriander.

KALE, CHICKPEA, FENNEL & DATE SALAD

 Serves 2-3

The trick to perfect chickpeas is soaking them overnight. I've always got some floating around in the pantry or precooked in the fridge, ready to go for this salad or a quick hummus.

> *2–3 kale leaves, coarsely chopped*
> *180 g (6 oz/1 cup) cooked chickpeas*
> *1 fennel bulb, trimmed and finely sliced*
> *1 large handful mint, leaves picked*
> *1 large handful parsley, leaves picked*
> *2 oranges, cut into segments*
> *100 ml (3½ fl oz) olive oil*
> *juice of 1 orange*
> *6 dates, quartered lengthways*
> *30 g (1 oz/¼ cup) walnut halves (optional)*

Put the kale, chickpeas, fennel, mint, parsley and orange segments in a large bowl and toss to combine.

Drizzle with the olive oil and orange juice, and season with salt and pepper.

Garnish with the dates and walnuts.

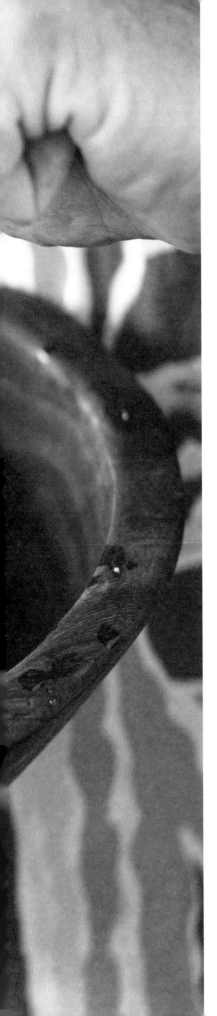

TRIPLE-GRAIN HIPSTER SALAD WITH SALMON

Serves 2

We love what we do, but we don't take ourselves too seriously. We understand the importance of a good laugh – even if it's at ourselves! This salad is full of every hipster ingredient we could think of, and, even though we might be poking a bit of fun, it really is super tasty and healthy.

100 ml (3½ fl oz) coconut oil
½ teaspoon minced garlic
½ teaspoon minced red chilli
½ teaspoon minced fresh ginger
½ onion, sliced
4 kale leaves (finely sliced)
40 g (1½ oz/⅓ cup) cooked quinoa (see page 240)
50 g (1¾ oz/⅓ cup) cooked wild rice
40 g (1½ oz/⅓ cup) cooked pearl barley
200 g (7 oz) salmon fillet
50 ml (1½ oz/2½ tablespoons) vegetable oil

To make the salad, heat the coconut oil in a medium heavy-based saucepan over medium heat. Add the garlic, chilli, ginger and onion and cook for 5 minutes, or until the onion is tender but not coloured. Add the sliced kale and cook for 3 minutes, or until wilted down. Add the quinoa, wild rice and pearl barley, and mix well. Remove from the heat, season with salt and pepper, and set aside.

To cook the salmon, pat it dry and season with salt on all sides.

Heat the vegetable oil in a non-stick frying pan over medium-high heat. Add the salmon, skin-side down, and apply pressure to the fish with a spatula for about 30 seconds to stop the fish curling up and keep the skin in contact with the pan. Cook for 4–5 minutes, or until skin is crisp. Turn the salmon and cook, covered, for 4–5 minutes for medium, or until cooked to your liking.

Serve the salmon with the salad on the side.

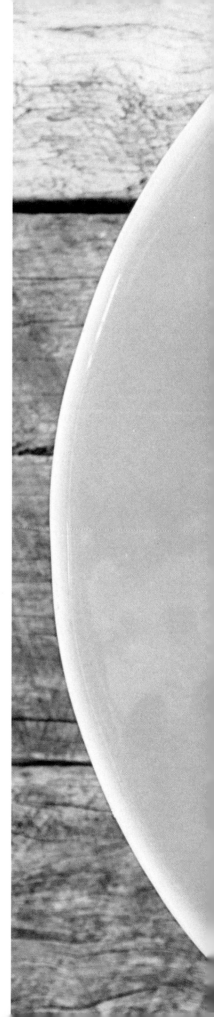

BEETROOT QUINOA RISOTTO   Serves 1-2

Sick of stirring your risotto for half an hour while it cooks on the stove? This recipe takes no time at all and is a great way to use up any extra cooked quinoa.

Side note: If you don't have extra cooked quinoa in your fridge, you should! It's such a handy thing to have ready to throw into salads, soups and stews, or make it into porridge or bircher.

> 1 large beetroot, skin on
> 1 tablespoon coconut oil
> ½ onion, finely diced
> 1 garlic clove, finely diced
> ½ red chilli, finely diced (keep the seeds if you
>   like it hot)
> 2 sprigs thyme, leaves picked, plus extra to serve
> 1 bay leaf
> 120 g (4 oz/1 cup) cooked quinoa (see page 240)
> 125 ml (4 fl oz/½ cup) vegetable stock (see page 240)
> 100 g (3½ oz) parmesan cheese, finely grated
> 100 g (3½ oz) goat's cheese
> ½ cup almonds, finely chopped

Preheat the oven to 200°C (400°F). Wrap the beetroot in foil and bake for 45 minutes, or until the beetroot is tender and easily pierced with a skewer. Coarsely chop the beetroot and set aside.

Heat the oil in a medium saucepan over medium heat. Add the onion, garlic, chilli, thyme and bay leaf, and cook until onion is tender but not coloured.

Meanwhile, place beetroot in a food processor and process until smooth, adding a little water if you need to get the puree moving.

Once the onion is tender, add quinoa, stock and beetroot puree to the saucepan and cook until the liquid has reduced by two-thirds. Add parmesan cheese and stir through. Season with salt and pepper.

Serve in a bowl sprinkled with thyme, goat's cheese and almonds.

Guy: I love to free dive off Flat Rock in North Bondi with my brother, Clint, and our mates. We started diving when I got Clint a spear gun for Christmas one year, then got jealous and bought myself one too!

You get so addicted to being underwater. We have been diving for a few years now, and while I'm by no means a pro, we can be down there for three to four minutes at a time. When you're in amongst it like that, swimming with the fish, it's a different world. At Bondi on a good current and when the water is clear, you can see 20 metres (over 21 yards).

I love finding good schools of fish and just watching them move. Fish are curious – when you're down at their level and if you're moving slowly, just in the right way, they will actually come over and check you out. It's hard to describe what it feels like having a school of 200 or so kingfish swimming around you.

The best thing about spearing is it's more sustainable than any other type of fishing – you can select the exact species and specimen you're going to take.

Kingfish arrive as the warm water currents flow through. We look for schools with a good number of legal-sized fish, then only take what we will eat.

You can eat a fresh kingy as sashimi right there on the rocks, but I love to make ceviche or grill a fish steak or put the whole fish on the barbecue for a big cook-up with mates.

Bondi has lots to offer – lobsters, kingfish, sand whiting, bonito, Aussie salmon, bream, squid and a plethora of other species both pelagic and local.

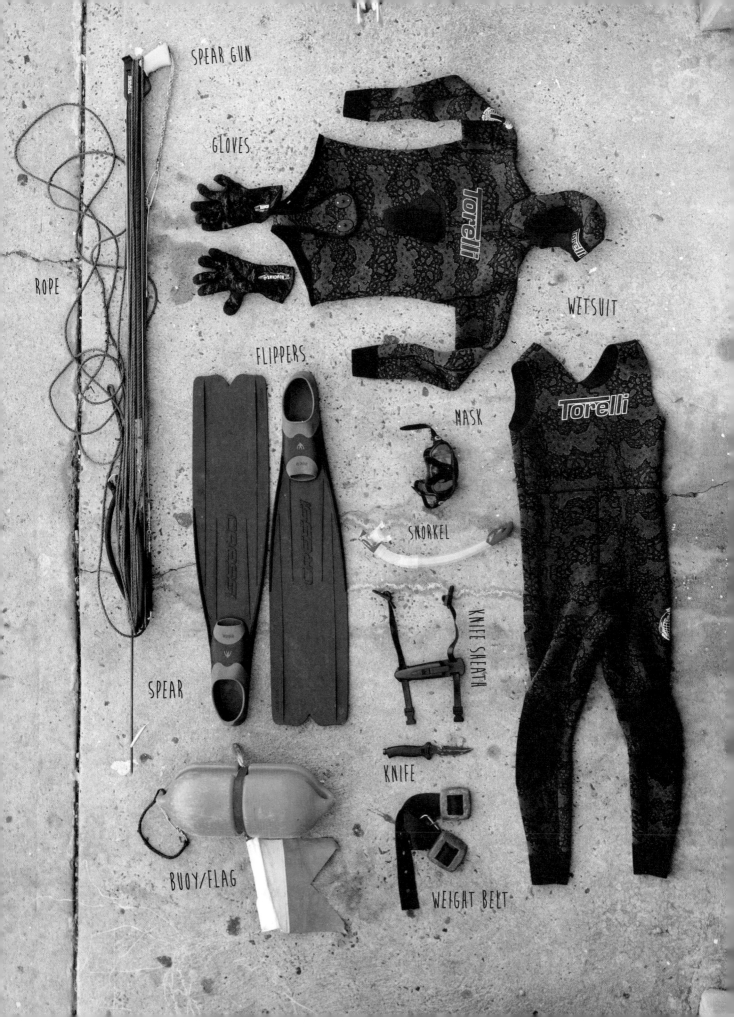

SPEAR GUN

GLOVES

ROPE

WETSUIT

FLIPPERS

MASK

Torelli

SNORKEL

KNIFE SHEATH

SPEAR

KNIFE

BUOY/FLAG

WEIGHT BELT

SUSTAINABLE FISHING

Today our oceans need more care than at any other time in human history. With overfishing of important species, unacceptable bio-catch wiping out vast numbers of other species and super trawlers emptying our oceans, we should view eating seafood as a privilege.

Next time you are buying fish or shellfish there are a few simple things you can do to make your seafood choices more sustainable – in other words, to make as little impact as possible on fish populations and the oceans that support them:

* Always try to eat local. In Australia, a staggering 70 per cent of seafood consumed is caught overseas. Look for local species and seafood caught in Australian waters.

* Buy directly from fishmongers – the more directly you can source your food, the better. Get to know your local fishmonger so you can get a feel for what fish are being caught locally.

* Is that species overfished? If so, look for an alternative.

* Ask if the fish is a deep-sea, slow-growing or long-lived species. If it is, it's more vulnerable to overfishing.

* And finally, where possible, buy whole fish and use the leftovers for fish stock and broth (see page 236).

VANILLA, CITRUS & FENNEL CURED SALMON

Serves 6

I fell in love with cured and smoked fish on bagels while I was in New York for a segment on NBC's Today Show, *and this recipe never fails to take me back. The fresh flavours make it perfect for a lazy Sunday brunch.*

220 g (7¾ oz/1 cup) sugar
130 g (4½ oz/1 cup) salt
zest of 2 lemons
zest of 2 oranges
zest of 3 limes
1 vanilla bean, split and seeds scraped
1 tablespoon black peppercorns, toasted
1 tablespoon fennel seeds, toasted
1 side (2 kg/4 lb 6½ oz) de-boned salmon fillet, skin off
lemon wedges, to serve
crispy bread or bagels, to serve

LEMON SOUR CREAM SPREAD
250 g (9 oz/1 cup) sour cream
1 tablespoon capers, drained
juice of 1 lemon
1 teaspoon dried chilli flakes

HERB SALAD
⅓ cup mint leaves
⅓ cup parsley leaves
⅓ cup coriander (cilantro) leaves
⅓ cup chopped dill
⅓ cup sliced spring onions (scallions)
1 tablespoon olive oil

To make the curing mixture, put the sugar, salt, lemon, orange and lime zest, vanilla seeds, toasted black pepper and fennel seeds in a medium bowl and mix well.

Spread half of the curing mixture in the base of a container large enough to accommodate the salmon. Put the salmon on top and pack the remaining curing mixture on top to completely cover it.

Cover the container and put in the fridge to cure overnight or for up to 12 hours (any longer and I find the salmon dries out).

Wash the cured salmon under cold running water. Pat it dry with paper towel, wrap in plastic wrap and store in the fridge for up to 2 weeks, slicing the salmon as you need it.

To make the lemon sour cream spread, put the sour cream, capers, lemon juice and chilli in a bowl. Season with salt and pepper and mix until combined.

To make the herb salad, put the mint, parsley, coriander, dill and spring onion in a medium bowl. Mix gently, sprinkle over the olive oil, season with salt and pepper and toss to coat.

To serve, slice the salmon super finely and lay it out on a large chopping board. Dollop on the lemon sour cream spread and scatter over the herb salad. Put lemon wedges and crispy bread or bagels on the side and you're ready to roll.

PUCKO GOING DEEP!!

SUMMER WATERMELON CEVICHE SALAD Serves 4

Ceviche is one of our favourite ways to serve fresh fish. It requires no heat because the fish 'cooks' as it marinates in the acidic citrus juices. The citrus also gives the fish the most unbelievably refreshing flavour and tenderises it, making it melt in your mouth.

300 g (10½ oz) whiting or any white-fleshed fish, cut into 2 cm (¾ inch) cubes
200 g (7 oz) watermelon, cut into 2 cm (¾ inch) cubes
250 g (9 oz) cherry tomatoes, halved if large
½ avocado, sliced
100 g (3½ oz) rocket (arugula)
6 slices prosciutto, torn, to serve

MARINADE
juice of 2 lemons
juice of 3 limes
juice of 2 oranges
1 red chilli, seeds discarded, finely chopped
1 red onion, finely chopped
1 tablespoon finely grated fresh ginger
2 tablespoons coconut cream
1 large handful coriander (cilantro) leaves, coarsely chopped

To make the marinade, put the juices, chilli, onion, ginger, coconut cream and half the coriander in a medium bowl and mix to combine. Add the fish and toss to coat. Cover and refrigerate for 1 hour.

Put the watermelon, tomato, avocado, rocket and remaining coriander in a large bowl. Toss gently, add the marinated fish and toss gently again.

Arrange the salad on a serving platter and scatter over the torn prosciutto.

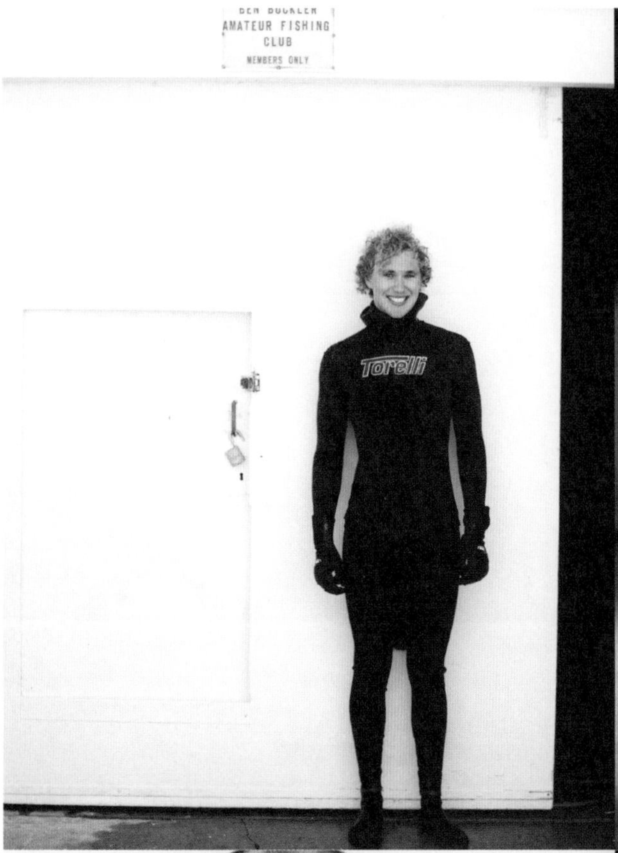
AMATEUR FISHING
CLUB
MEMBERS ONLY
Torelli

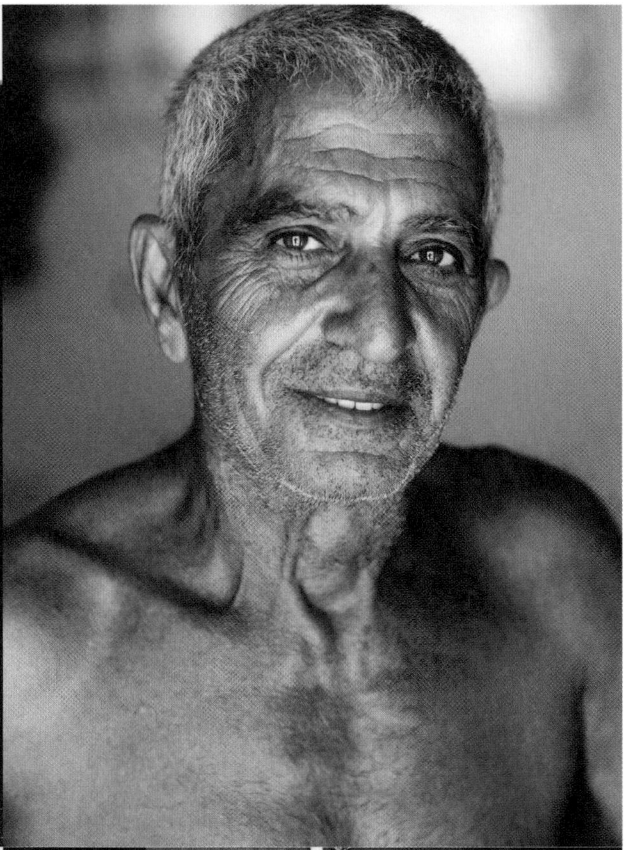

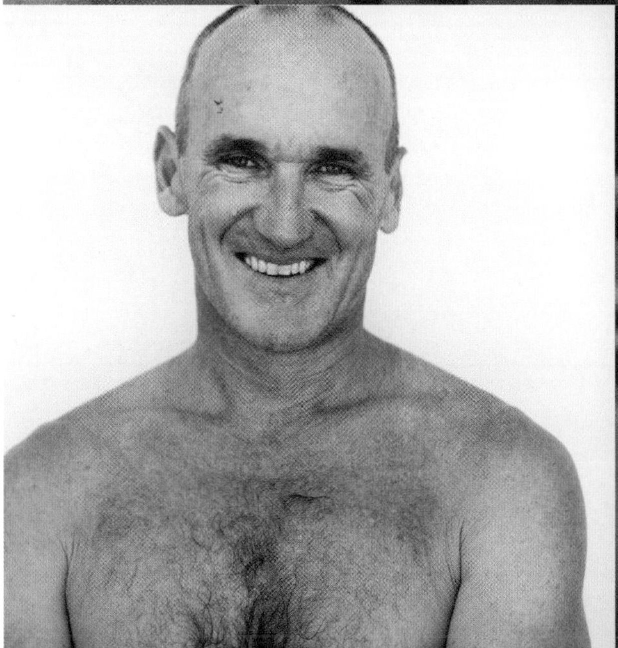

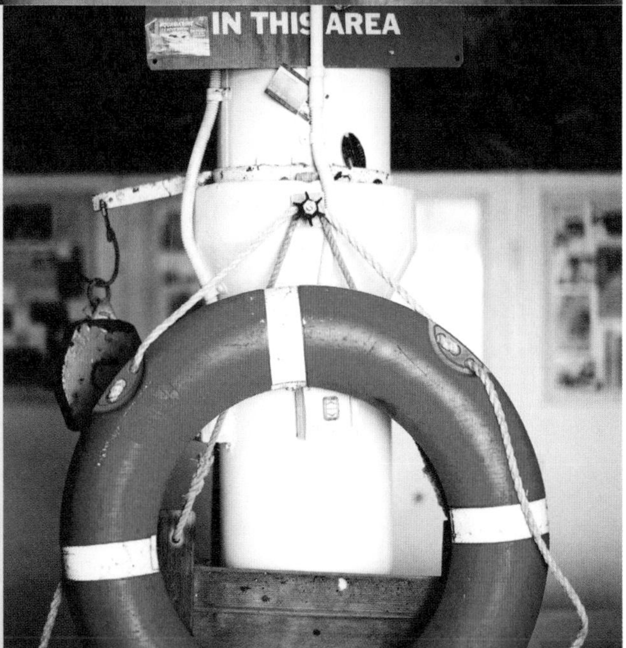
IN THIS AREA

STEAMED MUSSELS WITH KALE PESTO & OLIVE TOAST

Serves 4-5

Mussels are the ultimate sharing food, but when these mussels hit the table, 'sharing' takes on a new meaning – all manners go out the door, the bread starts flying and it's every man and woman for themselves!

1 kg (2 lb 4 oz) mussels
150 ml (5 fl oz) olive oil
1 onion, diced
1 garlic clove, minced
1 red chilli, minced
80 ml (2½ fl oz/⅓ cup) white wine
80 ml (2½ fl oz/⅓ cup) chicken stock
80 ml (2½ fl oz/⅓ cup) thin (pouring) cream
6 sprigs thyme, leaves picked
70 g (2½ oz/½ cup) cherry tomatoes, halved and squashed, or 125 g (4½ oz/½ cup) diced tomatoes
3 tablespoons kale pesto (see page 234)

OLIVE TOAST
1 tablespoon pitted olives, chopped
1 tablespoon chopped parsley
1 baguette
250 g (9 oz) butter, at room temperature

Clean the mussels by pulling the beard from the corner and purging in cold water for at least 5 minutes.

Heat the oil in a large heavy-based saucepan over high heat. Add the onion, garlic and chilli and cook for 6 minutes, or until the onion is soft. Add the wine, stock, cream and thyme, and bring to the boil.

Add the mussels and tomato, cover the saucepan with a lid and cook for 4–5 minutes, or until all the mussels have opened. Discard the ones that don't open.

To make the olive toast, preheat the oven to 180°C (350°F). Line a baking tray with baking paper.

Process the olives, parsley and butter in a food processor until combined. Slice the baguette on an angle, spread with the olive butter and put on the baking tray. Toast in the oven for 5–8 minutes, or until golden.

Serve the mussels in bowls with dollops of kale pesto and olive toast on the side.

SUPER SIMPLE SEAFOOD LASAGNETTE

Serves 2

I've always had a connection to the ocean, so when it comes to seafood I only ever eat sustainably or catch my own. I understand that cooking seafood can be intimidating for many people, so that's why I've created this super simple and tasty recipe.

6 dried or fresh lasagne sheets
100 ml (3½ fl oz) olive oil
½ teaspoon minced red chilli
½ teaspoon minced garlic
1 teaspoon fennel seeds
200 g (7 oz) cleaned and shelled prawns or
* other shellfish*
½ punnet cherry tomatoes
1 tablespoon salsa verde (see page 234)
zest and juice of 1 lemon (reserve juice for serving)

Place a medium pot of water on high heat, season with salt and bring to the boil. Place your lasagne sheets in the pot and cook for 6–7 minutes, or until al dente.

While the lasagne sheets are cooking, heat the olive oil in a medium saucepan over a medium heat. Add the chilli, garlic and fennel seeds, and cook for about 3 minutes, or until the garlic is soft and fragrant.

Add the prawns, cherry tomatoes and salsa verde, and cook for another 5 minutes.

Strain your pasta, then toss it through your sauce. Add lemon zest and season with salt and pepper.

Serve with a squeeze of lemon juice and enjoy.

SPICE-RUBBED SUSTAINABLE FISH SLIDERS

Serves 2-4

Sliders are simple, but perfecting them is a bit of an art. It's all about getting the three main components – the sauce, the filling and the bread – in the right ratio. We've got the sauce and filling covered, so all you need to do is get some fresh bread.

1 white fish fillet (for tips on buying sustainably, see page 113)
vegetable oil, for shallow-frying
4 fresh slider rolls
600 ml (21 fl oz) yoghurt tartar sauce (see page 234)
1 tomato, sliced

BONDI HARVEST SLIDER SLAW
⅓ red cabbage, coarsely grated
⅓ fennel bulb, coarsely grated
1 green apple, coarsely grated
⅓ red onion, finely sliced
1 large handful mint leaves
1 tablespoon pepitas (pumpkin seeds)
200 ml (7 fl oz) apple cider vinegar
50 ml (1½ fl oz/2½ tablespoons) olive oil

SPICE RUB
1 teaspoon coriander seeds
2 cardamom pods
1 teaspoon black peppercorns
1 teaspoon smoky paprika
2 teaspoons sea salt
1 teaspoon garlic powder
1 teaspoon dried oregano
1 teaspoon ground chilli

To make the slaw, put the cabbage, fennel, apple, onion, mint and pepitas in a large bowl. Put the vinegar and oil in a jar and shake together. Pour over the slaw and toss lightly. Set aside.

To make the spice rub, toast the coriander seeds and cardamom pods in a frying pan over medium-high heat. Using a mortar and pestle, pound and grind together the coriander, cardamom, peppercorns, paprika, salt, garlic powder, oregano and chilli.

Season the fish with the spice rub. Heat a little oil in a non-stick frying pan over medium heat. Pan-fry the fish for 5 minutes, flip and cook the other side for 5 minutes, or until cooked through.

I believe slider-building is a very personal thing, so gather together your rolls, fish, tartar sauce, slaw and tomato, and put together the slider of your dreams!

Super tasty
Fish sliders

BEER-BATTERED FISH & PUMPKIN CHIPS

Serves 4-5

After I've had an epic dive and filled my esky with fresh fish, I love calling mates to the café for a feed. For the best beer-battered fish, you need a few things: fresh fish, good-quality beer, my special infused salt, and lots of love.

220 g (7¾ oz/1¾ cups) self-raising flour
1 teaspoon sea salt
1 teaspoon freshly ground black pepper
1 teaspoon grated lemon zest
1 teaspoon lemon thyme leaves
375 ml (13 fl oz/1½ cups) beer
vegetable oil, for deep-frying
1 kg (2 lb 4 oz) white fish fillets
lime or lemon wedges, to serve

INFUSED SALT
1 tablespoon fennel seeds
½ tablespoon black peppercorns
2 teaspoons dried thyme
zest of 1 lemon
zest of 1 orange
130 g (4½ oz/1 cup) sea salt

PUMPKIN CHIPS
1 kg (2 lb 4 oz) butternut pumpkin (squash),
*   cut into 2 cm (¾ inch) thick fingers*
½ teaspoon ground cumin
½ teaspoon dried chilli
½ teaspoon salt
2 tablespoons coconut oil, melted

To make the batter, put the flour, salt, pepper, lemon zest and thyme leaves in a large bowl and mix to combine. Gradually add the beer, whisking continuously until combined and smooth. Set aside.

To make the pumpkin chips, preheat the oven to 200°C (400°F) and line a baking tray with baking paper. Put the pumpkin, cumin, chilli, salt and coconut oil in a large bowl and toss to coat the pumpkin well. Put the pumpkin on the tray and cook for 40 minutes, or until soft and golden brown.

To make the infused salt, heat a small frying pan over medium heat. Add the fennel seeds and peppercorns and toast for 5 minutes, until fragrant. Transfer to a food processor with the thyme and zest and process until combined. Or use a mortar and pestle to pound the ingredients for 5 minutes, or until combined. Combine with the sea salt and store in an airtight container.

Put 8 cm (3¼ inches) vegetable oil in a deep-fryer or large saucepan over high heat and heat to 190°C (375°F) (use a thermometer or just dip in a wooden spoon and when bubbles start to form around it, you're ready to roll). Line a plate with paper towel.

Dip two pieces of fish into the beer batter to completely coat it. Shake off any excess batter and submerge the fish in the hot oil. Deep-fry for 3–4 minutes, or until golden brown.

Transfer the cooked fish to the plate and repeat with the remaining fish.

Spread out this morning's newspaper and serve the fish and pumpkin chips on top, sprinkled with the infused salt and with lime or lemon wedges on the side.

Raw
Green
Smoothie
$11

Acai
Frappe
$9

Wine,
Beer
+
Cider

Young
Drinking
Coconuts
$5

Golden
Smoothie
$11

GRILLED CHIMICHURRI PRAWNS

 Serves 2

Mark is somewhat obsessed with chimichurri – the mere mention of it makes his face light up – so this is one of Mark's favourite recipes because we use chimichurri to marinate the prawns and then as a sauce to serve them with! Leave the shells on the prawns because they help protect the delicate flesh from the intense heat of the barbecue, so you'll get a juicer and tastier result.

> *1 firmly packed cup chopped parsley*
> *1 firmly packed cup chopped coriander (cilantro)*
> *½ firmly packed cup chopped oregano*
> *1 garlic clove, finely chopped*
> *200 ml (7 fl oz) extra virgin olive oil*
> *1½ tablespoons red wine vinegar*
> *1 tablespoon balsamic vinegar*
> *small pinch of dried chilli*
> *zest of 1 lemon*
> *6 green king prawns, shells intact*
> *lemon wedges, to serve*

To make the chimichurri, put the parsley, coriander, oregano, garlic, oil, vinegars, chilli, and zest in a small bowl. Season with salt and pepper and mix.

Spoon half the chimichurri over the prawns, cover and allow to marinate for at least 5 hours in the fridge. Reserve the remaining chimichurri for serving.

Preheat the barbecue grill to medium heat. Cook the prawns for 5 minutes, turning them continuously, or until they are coloured.

Put the prawns on a clean plate and serve drizzled with the reserved chimichurri and lemon wedges on the side.

WHOLE LEMON MYRTLE BARBECUED FISH & SALSA IN LETTUCE CUPS

The barbecue is a classic part of Australian beach culture. My brother and I will often spend the day out on the water fishing, then come home, marinate a beautiful kingfish or Aussie salmon and invite friends over for a barbecue. Cooking fish in a foil parcel allows it to steam beautifully, so you're left with soft and flaky flesh packed full of flavour.

1 whole fish
4 lemon myrtle leaves or 2.5 cm
  (1 inch) piece lemongrass
2 lemons, cut into round
  slices
1 kg (2 lb 4 oz) bok choy
  or kale
water and flesh of 1 young
  coconut
1 cos or iceberg lettuce

CURRY PASTE
1 teaspoon coriander seeds
1 teaspoon cumin
½ small onion, coarsely
  chopped

3 lemon myrtle leaves or
  2 cm (¾ inch) piece lemongrass
3 cm (1¼ inch) piece fresh ginger
4 red chillies (keep the seeds if
  you like it hot)
5 coriander (cilantro) roots
2 garlic cloves
2 tablespoons sesame oil
2 tablespoons coconut oil

SALSA
1 avocado, diced
1 large handful mint, leaves
  picked and chopped
1 red chilli, finely chopped
80 ml (2½ fl oz/¾ cup) lemon juice

To make the curry paste, heat a frying pan over medium-high heat and toast the coriander seeds and cumin for 10 minutes, until fragrant.

Put the toasted spices, onion, lemon myrtle leaves, ginger, chillies, coriander roots, garlic and oils in a food processor and process to a coarse paste, or pound using a mortar and pestle for 10–15 minutes.

Clean the fish and dry with paper towel. Rub about 1 tablespoon of the curry paste all over and inside the fish. Cover and put in the fridge to marinate for 4–12 hours (but no longer).

Preheat the barbecue to medium or the oven to 180°C (350°F).

Lay a long strip of foil twice as long as the whole fish on a clean bench. Lay the lemon myrtle leaves and lemon slices halfway along the foil. Put the bok choy over the lemon and place the fish on top.

Fold the sides of the foil up to create a pocket. Open the coconut and add 200 ml (7 fl oz) coconut water and the coconut flesh to the foil parcel. Close and seal the foil parcel tightly so there are no gaps, and double wrap with more foil if needed.

Put the fish parcel on the barbecue or in the oven and close the lid or door. Cook for 20–25 minutes. Remove the fish parcel from the barbecue or oven. Set it aside to rest for 5 minutes.

To make the salsa, combine all the ingredients in a bowl and season with salt and pepper.

Cut the stalk from the lettuce and gently pull away the large leaves to create lettuce cups.

Open the parcel and flake the fish away from the bone. Fill the lettuce cups with the fish and salsa.

 Serves 3

WHOLE WHITING BAKED IN PROSCIUTTO JACKETS WITH CHERRY TOMATOES

This is such a simple recipe, but one of our favourites. To be honest, the quantities we've provided are just a guide so you can play around and have fun with it. Can't get your hands on whiting? Get friendly with your fishmonger and ask him for a good alternative. Whole sardines would be tasty but you might need to reduce the cooking time a little.

250 g (9 oz) cherry tomatoes
2 red chillies, finely sliced
2 garlic cloves, squashed
4 sprigs thyme
1 bay leaf
30 g (1 oz) butter or 25 ml (¾ fl oz) coconut oil
1 lemon, sliced
pinch of sea salt
50 ml (1½ fl oz/2½ tablespoons) white wine
6 slices prosciutto
1 large handful parsley, coarsely chopped
1 large handful coriander (cilantro), coarsely chopped
3 whole whiting, cleaned

Preheat oven to 220°C (425°F). Line a large baking tray with baking paper.

Put the cherry tomatoes in the tray. Throw in the chilli, garlic, thyme, bay leaf, butter, lemon, sea salt and wine.

Lay 2 slices of prosciutto, slightly overlapping, on a flat surface. Top with one-third of the parsley and coriander and one of the fish. Wrap the fish in the prosciutto slices and put in the baking tray. Repeat twice more with the remaining prosciutto, herbs and fish.

Cook for 20 minutes, or until the prosciutto is crispy and the fish is cooked through.

Serve the fish parcels with the cherry tomatoes.

Mark: Like many locals, Guy and I have both come from outside the Bondi bubble – Guy from Bowral and me from Wagga Wagga. Being country boys, we both grew up with a close connection to the land and farming.

Coming from a long line of farmers on both sides of my family, I had the privilege of growing up with a clear understanding of where food comes from and the rewards and hardships involved in producing it.

It was my grandparents who really taught me how to appreciate food. I have a vivid memory of trapping rabbits with Pa for Nan to cook up for dinner, picking tomatoes for Nan's tomato relish (famous in CWA circles) and milking the cow early in the morning. When we were picked up, we went home with a bootload of produce.

Their lifestyle was about making use of everything, from nose to tail, and meals came direct from paddock to plate.

After leaving the family farm to make my own discoveries, I continued to feel a connection with the land but increasingly lost a connection with the food I was eating. Frustrated by this, I set out to change it and, in doing so, met Guy and created Bondi Harvest to help others find a real and meaningful connection with food.

BONDI SURFING

Guy: Surfing is such an important part of the day for us. It's where we find release from the busy kitchen, and where we get a chance to catch up with mates.

The Bondi wave depends on the sand banks. Sometimes, when you get the perfect combination of banks and swell hit, Bondi can really put it together. But the thing about surfing in Bondi is it's crowded – you're more dodging than surfing. So if you want an uncrowded wave, Bondi's not your beach. For us, it ends up being more about having a laugh than a good session.

In summer after we surf we love to head to the grassy knoll at North Bondi or a buddy's rooftop for a barbecue. Sharing meals with friends is what it's all about – it's where community begins, where conversations start and where good vibes are created.

When barbecuing, I love to cook on coals because the smoky flavours it creates are just so good. If you want to give it a go, you don't need all the expensive gear to create a great coal barbecue.

We usually make our coals in a brazier then transfer them over to under the grill, which is propped up using a bunch of old bricks. A good rule is to have your grill about 20 cm (8 inches) above the coals, and make sure you have a hot side and a medium side.

BUYING MEAT ETHICALLY

Meat is more often than not the chief element in a main course, and frequently the pièce de résistance of a meal. So when selecting meat, it's important to keep a few things in mind — where the meat came from, how it was raised and what you plan to do with it. For us, buying ethically is important. We believe that when you purchase mindfully, you can enjoy your meat even more when it's time to eat.

Sustainability is part of it, too. When animals are raised ethically, environmental protection is an important characteristic of its production. And this is where your local butcher really shines, as they will be able to answer questions about the meat — the region it came from, whether it was ethically raised and if it's certified organic. With this information (which the big supermarket chains often can't supply) on board, you can make informed choices, and increase your enjoyment of cooking and eating the meat, too.

Here's some terminology that might help you make your choices:

Grain-fed beef: For an animal to be classified as grain-fed, they must have been fed in an accredited feedlot for a required number of days. The minimum is 60 days, ranging through to 300+ for Wagyu export markets. The grain improves the quality and tenderness of the meat by increasing the marbling. Grain-fed meat is perfect for adding your own flavours and for cooking over smoky coals.

Grass-fed beef: For meat to be classified as grass fed, the animals need to spend their entire life grazing pastures. Typically, grass-fed meat has a tougher texture than grain-fed meat, but it has more flavour, which comes from the grasses the cattle have been grazing. The flavour varies, depending on the quality of the season, with less rainfall resulting in a decrease in feed quality.

Eating ethically means doing something with every cut of meat so nothing from the animal is wasted. At Bondi Harvest we practise responsible meat-buying, and cook using nose-to-tail principles. Look past the most common (and most expensive) cuts of meat and think about using the secondary cuts that are perfect for slow-cooking. Try bone marrow, kidneys and trotters — they sound scary, but cooking with them is easier and more delicious than you think!

CHOPPED CHICKEN SALAD Serves 3

I first made this salad in LA for some mates after an epic surfing session at Malibu Pier, so, for me, this salad's got good vibes all through it. It's the dressing in this salad that makes it awesome: lots of citrus and a mix of nuts and seeds to give it some real texture.

> *1 chicken breast*
> *1 teaspoon fennel seeds*
> *1 head cos lettuce, chopped*
> *1 avocado, chopped*
> *½ red onion, chopped*
> *150 g salami, chopped*
> *150 g gruyère cheese, chopped*
> *1 large handful mint, leaves picked*
>
> *DRESSING*
> *125 ml (4 fl oz/½ cup) olive oil*
> *2 tablespoons pepitas (pumpkin seeds)*
> *30 g (1 oz/¼ cup) pecans, chopped*
> *juice of 1 lemon*
> *juice of 1 lime*

Fill a medium saucepan with room-temperature water, add chicken breast and fennel seeds, and place over medium heat. Bring to a gentle simmer, and poach chicken for about 15–20 minutes, or until chicken is cooked through.

Meanwhile, in a large bowl, add lettuce, avocado, onion, salami, cheese and mint, and toss.

In another bowl, combine dressing ingredients and mix well.

To serve, pour dressing over salad and toss to coat well. Top with the diced poached chicken.

HERB-CRUSTED CHICKEN ROULADE WITH QUINOA SALAD

Serves 2-3

This recipe is great for two things: cooking super succulent chicken, and impressing friends with your French cooking skills!

Just remember, the key to perfect poached chicken is to put your chicken into cold water, and bring the water to a simmer slowly. It should take about 25–30 minutes to bring it to a simmer.

> 1 chicken breast
> 1 large handful parsley, leaves picked
> 1 large handful coriander (cilantro), leaves picked
> 2 long red chillies, finely chopped
> 1 garlic clove, finely chopped
> sea salt, for sprinkling
> 5 button mushrooms, finely chopped
> 1 avocado, chopped, to serve
> 1 tomato, chopped, to serve
>
> *QUINOA*
> 200 g (7 oz) quinoa
> 500 ml (17 fl oz/2 cups) chicken stock (see page 238)
> 1 garlic clove, coarsely chopped
> 2 red chillies, coarsely chopped
> 2 bay leaves

To make quinoa, in a medium saucepan over medium-high heat, bring quinoa, stock, garlic, chilli and bay leaves to the boil. Simmer for 12–15 minutes, or until quinoa is tender.

Meanwhile, to make chicken roulade, butterfly the chicken breast by cutting through it horizontally, but not all the way through. Flatten it out and lay it on a few layers of plastic wrap on a flat surface. Fold the plastic wrap over the chicken and roll a rolling pin over it until it is just under 1 cm (½ inch) thick.

In a bowl, mix the parsley, coriander, chilli and garlic. Spread the herb mix over a flat surface, and sprinkle with sea salt. Unwrap the chicken from the plastic wrap, and put the plastic wrap to one side. Lay the chicken flat over the herb mix, and press it into the mix to coat it well on one side.

Place the chicken back on the plastic wrap, herbed side down, place mushrooms in the centre, and roll the chicken around the mushrooms. Twist the ends of the plastic wrap to secure, and then wrap it in foil.

Place foil-wrapped roulade in a medium saucepan with cold water, and heat over a medium-low heat to bring to a gentle simmer. Simmer for 5 minutes. Remove roulade from the water and rest it in its wrappings for about 15 minutes.

Unwrap the foil, slice off one end of the plastic wrap and squeeze the roulade out. Slice into 2–3 cm (¾–1¼ inch) slices.

Serve with quinoa, avocado and tomato.

JERK CHICKEN

*When it's all about sharing an epic feed with mates, these chicken drumsticks
are the go. I like to serve them on a large chopping board with a side bowl of
super tasty pineapple salsa, because they're meant to be messy and enjoyed
with some beers in the sun after an afternoon of summer shenanigans . . .*

2 kg (4 lb 8 oz) chicken drumsticks, wings or whole
   butterflied chicken

JERK MARINADE
1 onion, coarsely chopped
3 cm (1¼ inch) piece fresh ginger, finely grated
3 jalapenos
1 teaspoon ground cinnamon
1½ teaspoons ground allspice
125 ml (4 fl oz/½ cup) spiced rum or coconut water
1½ tablespoons dark brown sugar
1½ tablespoons caster (superfine) sugar
100 g (3½ oz) barbecue sauce
1 handful thyme, leaves picked
4 coriander (cilantro) roots

PINEAPPLE SALSA
300 g (10½ oz) pineapple, cut into 2 cm (¾ inch) thick batons
1 avocado, diced
1 red onion, diced
1 small handful mint, leaves finely chopped
1 small handful coriander (cilantro), leaves finely chopped
1 jalapeno, finely chopped
1 garlic clove, finely chopped
zest of 3 limes
juice of 1 orange
50 ml (1½ fl oz/2½ tablespoons) olive oil

To make the marinade, put all the ingredients in a food processor and process
until combined.

Put the chicken in a baking dish or ziplock plastic bag. Add the Jerk marinade
and massage into the chicken. Cover or seal and put in the fridge overnight
to marinate.

Preheat half the grill to medium-high heat. Leaving the spice rub on the chicken,
put it on the grill and cook for 5–8 minutes, or until the skin begins to colour and
char. Turn the chicken and continue moving it on the grill for 5 minutes, or until it
is caramelised and evenly coloured.

Reduce the heat to medium-low, close the lid and continue to cook for 10–15
minutes, turning and checking every 5 minutes, until cooked or a thermometer
inserted into the meat reaches 75°C (165°F). Set aside to rest, covered with foil,
for 5 minutes before serving.

To make the pineapple salsa, clean the barbecue down, put the pineapple
batons on it and cook until charred and warmed through. Dice the pineapple and
transfer to a medium bowl. Add the avocado, onion, mint, coriander, jalapeno,
garlic and lime zest and mix gently. Shake together the orange juice and olive oil
and pour over the salsa. Season with salt and pepper and toss through.

Serve the chicken with salsa on the side, lots of napkins and a bowl for
the bones.

OUR NEW PLACE

HALOUMI TURKEY MEATBALLS IN SMOKY TOMATO SAUCE

Serves 3-4

It's simple: prep it, mash it, roll it, fry it and eat it. Sweet turkey, smoky sauce, chunks of salty haloumi – how can you lose? You can also use chicken mince for this recipe.

1 onion, finely diced
2 garlic cloves, minced
100 g (3½ oz) haloumi, finely diced
1 tablespoon dried oregano
30 g (1 oz/1 cup) chopped parsley, plus extra to serve
50 g (1¾ oz/½ cup) finely grated parmesan cheese
1 egg, whisked
450 g (1 lb) turkey mince
1 tablespoon olive oil
1 lemon, cut into wedges
sourdough bread, to serve

SMOKY TOMATO SAUCE
1 onion, finely diced
1 garlic clove, minced
½ red capsicum (pepper), diced
1 red chilli, diced (keep the seeds if you like it hot)
1 celery stick, diced
½ tablespoon fennel seeds
1 tablespoon smoked paprika
½ tablespoon tomato paste (concentrated purée)
425 g (15 oz) tin chopped tomatoes

To make the meatballs, put the onion, garlic, haloumi, oregano, parsley, parmesan cheese and egg in a large bowl and mix well. Break up the turkey mince, add to the bowl with salt and pepper to taste, and mix until well combined. Roll the mixture into 3–4 cm (1¼-1½ inch) round balls and refrigerate for 30 minutes or more.

Heat the olive oil in a medium saucepan over medium heat. Add the meatballs and cook, moving them around frequently, for 5 minutes, or until golden brown. Transfer to a bowl.

To make the smoky tomato sauce, using the same saucepan, cook the onion, garlic, capsicum, chilli, celery and fennel seeds for 7 minutes, until tender. Add the paprika and tomato paste and cook for 2 minutes. Reduce the heat to low, add the tomato and cook for 10 minutes to develop the flavours and reduce the sauce. Add the meatballs to the sauce and simmer for 5 minutes, or until tender and cooked through.

Transfer the meatballs and sauce to a serving bowl. Scatter over the extra parsley, and serve with lemon wedges and sourdough.

MOJO PORK TACOS WITH SWEET APPLE SLAW

Serves 4-5

Perfect with a couple of Coronas with lime wedges, these tacos make for the ultimate summer communal dining experience. The combination of hot, tangy and sweet flavours is amazing. Share them with your mates and they'll be your friends for life.

3 kg (6 lb 10 oz) pork loin
1 tablespoon olive oil
12 tortillas
1 teaspoon mixed
   dried herbs
3 avocados, sliced

MOJO MARINADE
1 large handful coriander
   (cilantro), leaves finely
   chopped
zest and juice of 2 oranges
zest and juice of 4 limes
zest and juice of 2 lemons
1 handful mint, leaves
   finely chopped
8 garlic cloves, crushed
15 g (½ oz/½ cup) fresh
   oregano leaves
1 teaspoon ground cumin
15 g (½ oz/½ cup) finely
   chopped parsley

200 ml (7 fl oz) olive oil
1 red chilli, finely chopped
   (keep the seeds if you like
   it hot)

APPLE SLAW
2 green apples, coarsely
   grated
⅓ red cabbage, coarsely
   grated
1 garlic clove, crushed
1 red chilli, finely chopped
   (keep the seeds if you
   like it hot)
8 spring onions (scallions),
   finely sliced
1 handful coriander
   (cilantro), leaves picked
300 ml (10½ fl oz) white wine
   vinegar or apple cider
   vinegar

Combine all of the marinade ingredients in a medium bowl.

Put the pork loin in a large ziplock bag with the marinade, seal and massage the marinade into the pork. Put the bag in the fridge and marinate for at least 5 hours or overnight.

Preheat the oven to 220°C (425°F).

Heat the oil in a large ovenproof frying pan over medium heat. Remove the pork from the bag and allow the excess marinade to drip away. Cook the pork, turning frequently, for 5 minutes, or until golden brown on all sides.

Put the pan in the oven and cook for 7 minutes, or until a thermometer inserted into the meat reads 62–65°C (143–149°F). Remove from the oven and rest for 10 minutes before slicing.

To make the apple slaw, put the apple, cabbage, garlic, chilli, spring onion and coriander in a medium bowl. Pour over the vinegar, season with salt and pepper and toss to combine.

Assembling a taco is a very personal thing so I'm not going to tell you how to make yours, but here's how I do mine.

I preheat the oven to 180°C (350°F). I wrap my tortillas in foil with the dry herbs and stick them in the oven.

I get my warm tortilla, put down a layer of avocado slices, then a layer of pork, and then spoon on the epic slaw. I wrap it up and there's no holding back.

So get in there like a shot of tequila and make a mess!

HERBED CORN & PARMESAN CRUMBED CHICKEN WITH LEMON KALE

Serves 2-3

We've done a Bondi Harvest spin on an old favourite to make the most epic chicken schnitzel you've ever had. First up, it's gluten free . . . Whaaaat!!?? Yep, and we've thrown in a bunch of fresh herbs and some parmesan cheese to really up the ante in the flavour department. And if there's any left over, it'll make the perfect post-surf sambo.

2 chicken breast fillets
1 cup corn crumbs
(available from natural and
health food stores, or you
can make your own by
processing cornflakes in
a food processor)
100 g (3½ oz/1 cup) grated
parmesan cheese
1 small handful parsley,
leaves picked
1 small handful mint, leaves
picked
½ handful thyme, leaves
picked
zest of 1 lemon
5 eggs, whisked
125 g (4½ oz/1 cup)
cornflour (corn starch)

vegetable or coconut oil, for
shallow-frying
lemon wedge, to serve

LEMON KALE
80 g (2¾ oz) butter or 80 ml
(2½ fl oz) coconut oil
1 leek, white part only,
finely sliced
1 red chilli, finely sliced
1 garlic clove, roughly
chopped
1 bunch kale, stalks
removed, leaves coarsely
chopped
juice of 1 lemon
80 ml (2½ fl oz) thin
(pouring) cream (optional)
1 handful mint, leaves picked

To butterfly the chicken, put one of the breasts flat on a clean chopping board, place a sharp knife on the side of the chicken and slice through the breast slowly to the other side but do not cut all the way through.

Fold out the chicken breast and place between two sheets of baking paper. Using a meat mallet or empty wine bottle, gently pound flat the chicken until it is all the same thickness. Repeat with the other chicken breast.

To make the crumbing mixture, put the corn crumbs, parmesan, parsley, mint, thyme and zest in a food processor with a blade attachment and process on high until combined and a crumb consistency. Alternatively, you can chop the herbs finely and mix with the crumbs and parmesan in a bowl.

Set out three bowls and use one each for the egg, cornflour and crumbing mixture.

Dip a butterflied chicken breast in the cornflour to coat it completely then gently shake off any excess, then into the egg mixture, and then into the corn crumbs, pressing the chicken down to cover it completely. Repeat with the remaining breast.

Heat enough oil (I use coconut oil) to generously cover the base of a large frying pan over medium heat. Add the crumbed chicken and cook for 4–5 minutes, or until golden brown. Carefully turn the chicken and repeat on the other side until cooked through. Set aside and cover with foil to keep warm.

To make the lemon kale, heat the butter or coconut oil in a medium saucepan over medium heat. Add the leek, chilli and garlic and allow to sweat down for 5 minutes, or until tender. Add the kale and cook for 3 minutes, or until it just collapses but is still a vibrant green. Remove the pan from the heat. Add the juice and cream, if using, and season with salt and pepper. Fold through the mint and serve with the crumbed chicken and lemon wedge.

SPICY LAMB KOFTA WITH LABNEH & ZA'ATAR

Serves 3-4

Bondi is a weird, wonderful and ever-evolving mix of different cultures and religions, which means for me – as a chef and food-lover – there's no shortage of inspiration, new people to meet and things to learn. This dish comes from the Middle Eastern end of the spectrum.

500 g (1 lb 2 oz) lamb mince
1 garlic clove, minced
1 red chilli, minced
1 tablespoon finely chopped spring onion (scallion)
1 tablespoon thyme leaves
1 teaspoon green peppercorns
1 teaspoon dried oregano
zest of 1 lemon
lemon wedges, to serve
flatbread, to serve

LABNEH
2 cups full-fat, unsweetened Greek-style yoghurt
½ teaspoon sea salt
½ teaspoon freshly ground black pepper

ZA'ATAR
1 cup dried oregano
1 cup dried thyme
1 cup dried marjoram
½ cup sesame seeds
½ cup salt
1 tablespoon freshly ground black pepper
zest of 1 lemon

To make the labneh, combine the yoghurt, salt and pepper in a bowl. Place a colander over a bowl or bucket, and line the colander with wet cheesecloth or a large coffee filter. Pour the yoghurt mixture into the cheesecloth, and pull up the sides and tie tightly with string or a rubber band to create a pouch. Put a plate and several heavy tins of food on top of the pouch to press out the liquid. Put in the fridge for 15 hours.

Soak wooden skewers in water overnight for the kofta.

To make the za'atar, combine all the ingredients in a bowl and transfer to an airtight container.

To make the kofta, put the lamb, garlic, chilli, spring onion, thyme, peppercorns, oregano and zest in a large bowl and mix for 5 minutes, until well combined.

Divide the mixture into 5 equal parts. Using clean damp hands, squeeze and shape one portion of the meat mixture along and around a skewer. Continue with the remaining meat and skewers then cover and put in the fridge for at least 1 hour.

Preheat the barbecue to medium.

Grill the kofta for 8–10 minutes, until coloured and cooked through.

Serve on a plate with the za'atar for sprinkling, lemon wedges for squeezing, and labneh and flatbread on the side.

BARBECUE BRISKET WITH PICKLED FENNEL

Serves 5-6

You've probably never thought of throwing some brisket on the barbie, but this recipe will totally convert you. It's all about giving this underrated cut the attention it deserves – let the dry marinade flavours penetrate and tenderise the brisket and I promise once it hits the barbecue, the aroma will blow your mind! And the pickled fennel? You won't believe how good it tastes either.

3 kg (6 lb 10 oz) beef brisket
brioche slider buns, to serve
apple slaw (see page 166),
  to serve
lemon wedges, to serve
aïoli (see page 232), to serve

PICKLED FENNEL
250 ml (9 fl oz/1 cup) apple
  cider vinegar
110 g (3¾ oz/½ cup) white
  sugar
5 whole cloves
1 teaspoon fennel seeds

1 bulb fennel, trimmed and
  sliced

SPICE MIXTURE
3 teaspoons garlic powder
3 teaspoons ground
  coriander
2 tablespoons smoked
  paprika
4 tablespoons dark brown
  sugar
5 tablespoons whole black
  peppercorns
100 g (3½ oz/¾ cup) sea salt

To make the pickled fennel, sterilise a large mason jar. Remove the lid and put it and the jar in a large saucepan of water over high heat. Bring to the boil and let it sit for 10–15 minutes. Put the jar and the lid on a clean tea towel to dry.

Put the vinegar, 250 ml (9 fl oz/1 cup) water, sugar, cloves and fennel seeds in a large saucepan over medium heat. Bring to a simmer, reduce the heat to low and stir to dissolve the sugar. Add the fennel to the saucepan with the pickling liquid and bring it back to a simmer. Cook for 7–8 minutes, or until the fennel is tender.

Transfer the fennel and liquid to the sterilised jar. Tap the jar as you pour in the liquid to release any air bubbles. Seal the jar well with its lid.

Fill a medium saucepan with water over high heat. Put the jar in the boiling water, turn the heat off and allow it to sit there for 20 minutes, to create a vacuum seal. Set aside the jar on a cloth to cool down completely.

Meanwhile, make the spice mixture for the brisket. Use a mortar and pestle or food processor to grind or process the garlic powder, coriander, paprika, brown sugar, black pepper and sea salt to a coarse powder.

Rub some of the spice mixture into the brisket on all sides, put in a ziplock bag or covered baking dish and add the remaining spice mixture. Put in the fridge and marinate for at least 5 hours or overnight.

Preheat the barbecue to high. Take the brisket out of the ziplock bag. The dry spice mixture will have drawn moisture from the meat, so give it a light wipe before placing it on the barbecue. Cook for 30 minutes, turning every 5 minutes, to create a beautifully dark colour and crust.

Reduce the heat to low and cook for 2½ hours, turning every 30 minutes and brushing with the remaining spice mixture every 10–20 minutes. Remove the brisket from the heat, wrap in foil and allow to rest for 20 minutes before slicing.

I like to serve this brisket on a massive platter with the pickled fennel, a few brioche slider buns, slaw, lemon wedges and aïoli.

The things you LOVE!

SLOW-COOKED LAMB SHOULDER ON SMASHED GREEN PEAS

Serves 4-5

I've cooked this recipe hundreds of times and I'm still amazed by how tasty and tender this lamb shoulder is. Give it the love it needs and the result is sooooo good.

1 tablespoon olive oil
2 kg (4 lb 8 oz) lamb shoulder
1 onion, coarsely chopped
1 garlic clove, finely chopped
1 carrot, coarsely chopped
1 large handful thyme, leaves picked
250 g (9 oz) tomato paste (concentrated purée)
4 litres (135 fl oz/16 cups) chicken stock
750 ml (26 fl oz/3 cups) red wine
125 g (4½ oz/½ cup) kale pesto (see page 234)
320 g (11¼ oz/2 cups) toasted almonds, to serve
thyme sprigs, to serve (optional)

SMASHED PEAS
65 g (2¼ oz/½ cup) green peas, cooked
1 handful mint, leaves picked
80 g (2¾ oz/⅓ cup) ricotta
3 small red chillies, minced

Preheat the oven to 175°C (345°F).

Heat the oil in a large frying pan over high heat. Add the lamb shoulder and cook for 10 minutes, turning, until golden brown.

Put the lamb shoulder in a baking dish with the onion, garlic, carrot, thyme, tomato paste and stock. Set aside.

Put the wine in a medium saucepan over high heat. Cook until reduced by three-quarters.

Pour the wine reduction over the lamb. Cover the baking dish with foil, sealing at the sides, and cook in the oven for 3 hours, or until the lamb is falling off the bone.

Remove the baking dish from the oven, carefully transfer the lamb to a large plate and smother with the pesto. Set aside.

Strain the braising liquid into a medium saucepan over high heat. Cook for 20 minutes, until reduced by two-thirds. Pour into a serving jug.

To make the smashed peas, put the peas, mint, ricotta and chilli in a bowl and combine well using a masher or a whisk. Smash it, taste it, then season it.

To serve, spread the smashed peas over the base of a large baking dish. Put the lamb on top. At the table, pour the reduced braising liquid over the lamb, scatter over the almonds and thyme sprigs, and let everyone dig in.

LAMB SHANKS WITH HOMEMADE POLENTA *Serves 4-5*

Don't be intimidated by the list of ingredients – this recipe is so easy and is worth stepping outside your comfort zone for. All it takes is a little time and care. And I reckon the anticipation you feel waiting for this dish to come out of the oven makes it just that little bit tastier.

You could also use oxtail instead of lamb shanks.

1 tablespoon olive oil
4 lamb shanks, or 1 kg (2 lb 4 oz) oxtail, cut into
   4 cm (1½ inch) slices
1 onion, coarsely chopped
2 garlic cloves, coarsely chopped
1 celery stick, coarsely chopped
1 tablespoon tomato paste (concentrated purée)
500 ml (17 fl oz/2 cups) red wine
1 litre (35 fl oz/4 cups) chicken stock
1 small handful thyme, leaves picked
1 tablespoon fennel seeds
½ tablespoon cumin seeds
1 tablespoon dried oregano
1 bay leaf
250 g (9 oz) walnuts, toasted
fresh oregano leaves, to serve (optional)

POLENTA
50 g (1¾ oz) butter
½ onion, diced
1 garlic clove, minced
400 g (14 oz/2 cups) corn kernels cut from the cob
100 ml (3½ fl oz) chicken stock
50 g (1¾ oz) parmesan cheese, grated (optional)

Preheat the oven to 180°C (350°F).

Heat the oil in a baking dish or medium ovenproof saucepan over medium-high heat. Add the lamb shanks and cook, turning frequently, until golden brown. Transfer to a plate.

Using the same baking dish or saucepan, add the onion, garlic and celery. Cook for 5 minutes, until tender. Add the tomato paste, wine, stock, thyme, fennel seeds, cumin seeds, oregano and bay leaf. Return the lamb shanks to the dish or saucepan. Stir to combine, cover with a lid and transfer the baking dish or saucepan to the oven. Cook for 3–4 hours, until the meat falls off the bone.

Transfer the lamb shanks to a plate. Strain the liquid from the baking dish into a small saucepan over medium heat. Cook the braising liquid for 30 minutes, or until thick and reduced by two-thirds and coating the back of a spoon.

To make the polenta, melt the butter in a medium saucepan over medium heat. Add the onion and garlic and cook for 5 minutes, or until tender. Add the corn and cook, stirring, for 5 minutes. Add the stock and cook for 20 minutes, until the corn has broken down and liquid has reduced. Season with salt, pepper and the parmesan cheese, if using.

Serve a spoonful of polenta on a plate with the braised lamb shanks and sauce on top. Garnish with the walnuts and fresh oregano.

DESSERTS

Guy: Life is too short not to have dessert, so just make it good and enjoy it! 'Real-world balance' is what I call it – why train hard and eat healthy if you can't enjoy the good things in life, like a slice of chocolate cake? I like to approach desserts much like I do life: with a yin and yang mind-set. There's a mix of healthy and not-so-healthy decadent desserts in this chapter, so you can pick something on the light side, or go all out for a special occasion. One thing I can promise is that whatever you choose, it'll be tasty as hell and you'll wish you made more!

*

Mark and Guy: Our approach is to start with the produce and invent from there. So, we check out what fruit is in season, and think about how we can take that flavour and enhance it even more.

We try to use natural sources of sugar wherever possible – honey, maple syrup and even stevia. This year we have been sourcing small-batch honey from local beekeepers – both urban and from the bush. It's incredible the diversity of flavour you get, from the unique taste of the flowering gum trees to the notes of aniseed from wild-growing fennel. The flavour of the honey changes throughout the year depending on what plants are flowering – makes sense, right?!

Our next short-term goal is to start our own bee hive so we'll be getting 100 per cent raw, straight-from-the-hive Bondi Harvest honey.

Tending bees is such a Zen thing to do. They force you to slow your movements and flow when you're working with them. They are the best pet you can have – you don't have to feed them but they feed you!

'WE DON'T WEAR JEANS THAT HAVE KNEES'

RAW CACAO ENERGY BALLS

Is chocolate your guilty pleasure? No need for the 'guilty' part any more. Chocolate fix sorted.

> 105 g (3½ oz/1 cup) 100 per cent raw cacao powder
> 400 g (14 oz/4 cups) almond meal
> 100 g (3½ oz/1 cup) protein powder
> 3 tablespoons honey
> 5 tablespoons coconut water
> 5 tablespoons desiccated coconut
> 3 tablespoons chia seeds

Put cacao powder, almond meal and protein powder in a food processor and buzz until combined. Add the honey and coconut water and buzz until a firm paste forms.

Roll tablespoonfuls of the mixture into about 10 balls. Mix the desiccated coconut and chia seeds in a small bowl. Roll the balls in the mixture to coat them and refrigerate in an airtight container for up to 2 weeks.

PEANUT, SEA SALT, CHIA SEED & CHAI DATE BALLS

Makes 10 balls

These should come with a warning: the mix of peanut and sea salt makes them addictive.

> 1 tablespoon chai leaves
> 12 pitted dates
> 3 tablespoons peanut butter (see page 228, 'Raw nut butter')
> 3 teaspoons 100 per cent raw cacao powder
> 150 g (5½ oz/1½ cups) almond meal
> 1 teaspoon sea salt
> 4 tablespoons chia seeds

Brew a cup of chai tea with 250 ml simmering water and chai leaves for 10 minutes.

Put the dates in a small bowl and pour the strained chai tea over them. Set aside to cool to room temperature.

Put the dates, peanut butter, cacao powder, almond meal, salt and 80 ml (2½ fl oz/⅓ cup) water in a food processor and blend until combined (I like it to still be a bit chunky).

Roll tablespoonfuls of the mixture into balls. Put the chia seeds in a bowl and roll the balls in them to coat. Store in an airtight container in the fridge for up to 2 weeks.

MOCHA PROTEIN ENERGY BALLS

Makes 10 balls

These tasty little treats are my alternative to chemical-filled energy drinks. They are all natural, full of energy and, most importantly, damn tasty. Once you've tried these, you'll never go back to the dark side.

10 pitted dates
80 ml (2½ fl oz/⅓ cup) hot espresso coffee
50 g (1¾ oz/½ cup) almond meal
1 tablespoon cocoa
2 tablespoons pea protein powder
1 tablespoon chia seeds
2 tablespoons honey
95 g (3¼ oz/1 cup) crushed almonds

Put the dates in a small bowl. Pour the hot coffee over the dates and set aside to soften and cool to room temperature.

Put the softened dates and coffee in a food processor and buzz until smooth. Add the almond meal, cocoa, protein powder, chia seeds and honey and process for 3 minutes, or until the mixture comes together.

Roll tablespoonfuls of the mixture into balls.

Put the crushed almonds in a small bowl. Roll the balls in the almonds to coat.

Store in an airtight container in the fridge for up to 2 weeks.

GOJI, LEMON, GINGER & ALMOND BALLS

Makes 10 balls

ZING is the perfect word to describe these. Full of lemon and ginger, they pack a vitamin C punch, making them the perfect treat for when your immune system needs a boost.

300 g (10½ oz/3 cups) almond meal
zest and juice of 2 lemons
1 teaspoon ginger juice (grate fresh ginger and
*   push it through a strainer to extract the juice)*
2 tablespoons goji berries
100 g (3½ oz/1 cup) protein powder
3 tablespoons honey
45 g (1½ oz/½ cup) desiccated coconut

Put the almond meal, lemon zest and juice, ginger juice, goji berries, protein powder and honey in a large bowl. Work the mixture together with clean hands until it binds.

Roll tablespoonfuls of the mixture into balls.

Put the desiccated coconut in a small bowl. Roll the balls in the coconut to coat.

Store in an airtight container in the fridge for up to 2 weeks.

MOCHA PROTEIN ENERGY BALL

PEANUT, SEA SALT, CHIA SEED & CHAI DATE BALL

GOJI, LEMON, GINGER & ALMOND BALL

RAW CACAO ENERGY BALL

RAW CARAMEL SLICE

 GF V Serves 8

Caramel slice might sound like a naughty treat, but it's not! This caramel slice is all about flavour with none of the bad stuff.

135 g (4¾ oz/½ cup) tahini (see page 228)
125 ml (4 fl oz/½ cup) maple syrup
250 ml (9 fl oz/1 cup) coconut oil
1 vanilla bean, split and seeds scraped

CHOC TOP
250 ml (9 fl oz/1 cup) coconut oil, melted
3 tablespoons agave syrup
3 tablespoons cocoa

BASE
160 g (5½ oz/1 cup) almonds
85 g (3 oz/½ cup) pitted dates
2 tablespoons coconut oil

To make the base, put the almonds, dates and coconut oil in a food processor and process until smooth. Press into a 35 cm x 13 cm (14 inch x 5 inch) slice tin lined with baking paper. Put in the fridge for 10 minutes to set.

Meanwhile, make the filling. Put the tahini, maple syrup, coconut oil and vanilla seeds in the food processor and process until smooth. Pour the mixture over the base and return to the fridge for 30 minutes to set.

To make the top chocolate layer, put the coconut oil, agave syrup and cocoa in a bowl and mix to combine. Pour the mixture over the filling and return to the fridge for 30 minutes to set.

On a hot summer's day, nothing is as refreshing as frozen fruity treats. These are our some of our favourite fruit whips – but really, all you need are some frozen fruits in the freezer and you're ready to roll. Get creative with textures and ingredients – nothing comes close to fresh in-season fruits and herbs from the backyard.

CACAO, PEANUT BUTTER & JELLY WHIP   Serves 2

> *3 frozen bananas, halved*
> *2 teaspoons 100 per cent raw cacao powder*
> *½ tablespoon honey*
> *2 tablespoons homemade peanut butter*
>   *(see page 228, 'Raw nut butter')*
> *⅓ cup hulled strawberries*
> *1 small handful almonds, to serve*
> *1 tablespoon toasted coconut, to serve*

Put the bananas, cacao powder and honey in a food processor and process until just smooth (don't overprocess or the banana will melt). Add the peanut butter and strawberries and pulse once or twice, just enough to swirl through.

If you can stop yourself from eating it all straight from the processor, put the mixture in a container with a lid and freeze for up to 2 months. If you like, you can give it another very quick buzz in the food processor when you want to eat it.

Sprinkle with almonds and toasted coconut to serve.

MIXED BERRY, BANANA, COCONUT & THYME WHIP Serves 2

> *70 g (2½ oz/½ cup) frozen mixed berries*
> *3 frozen bananas, halved*
> *flesh of 1 coconut, coarsely chopped*
> *½ tablespoon coconut cream*
> *½ tablespoon Greek-style yoghurt*
> *1 tablespoon honey*
> *½ teaspoon fresh thyme leaves*

Put all the ingredients in a food processor and process until just smooth (don't overprocess or the fruit will melt). Put the mixture in an airtight container and freeze. Store in the freezer for up to 4 months.

MINTY PINEAPPLE, COCOA, BANANA,
CHIA & ALMOND WHIP

MANGO, BANANA & PROTEIN WHIP

MIXED BERRY, BANANA, COCONUT & THYME WHIP

MANGO, BANANA & PROTEIN WHIP

Serves 2

> 2 frozen mango cheeks
> zest and juice of 1 lemon
> 1 tablespoon honey
> ½ teaspoon ginger juice (grate fresh ginger and push
>   through a strainer to extract the juice)
> 2 frozen bananas, halved
> 1 tablespoon protein powder

Put all the ingredients in a food processor and process until just smooth (don't overprocess or the fruit will melt). Resist the temptation to eat the mixture now and put it in an airtight container and freeze. Store in the freezer for up to 2 months. If you like, you can give it another very quick buzz in the food processor before you eat it.

MINTY PINEAPPLE, COCOA, BANANA, CHIA & ALMOND WHIP

Serves 2

> 3 frozen bananas, halved
> 1 cup frozen pineapple, coarsely chopped
> ½ cup mint leaves
> 1 tablespoon chia seeds
> 40 g (1½ oz/¼ cup) almonds
> 2 tablespoons cocoa

Put the banana and pineapple in a food processor and process until just smooth (don't overprocess or the fruit will melt). Add the mint, chia seeds, almonds and cocoa and pulse just until ground up and combined.

Have a quick taste and put the mixture in an airtight container and freeze. Store in the freezer for up to 2 months. If you like, you can give it another very quick buzz in the food processor before you eat it.

VANILLA, YOGHURT & COCONUT PANNA COTTA WITH HONEY NUT BRITTLE

 Makes 10

There's no substitute for flavour; it absolutely has to taste good.
The fact that this panna cotta is healthier than others is just a bonus.
Make sure to use a good-quality probiotic yoghurt.

7.5 g (¼ oz) gelatine leaves, or 12 g (½ oz/
* 4 teaspoons) powdered gelatine*
900 ml (30 fl oz) coconut milk
150 g (5½ oz) sugar
1 vanilla bean, split and seeds scraped
zest of 1 lemon
300 ml (10½ fl oz) almond milk
400 g (14 oz) natural yoghurt
200 g (7 oz) fresh berries, to serve

HONEY NUT BRITTLE
2 tablespoons honey
80 g (2¾ oz/½ cup) almonds, coarsely chopped
1 tablespoon dark brown sugar
1 tablespoon coconut oil or butter
½ teaspoon sea salt
2 sprigs thyme, leaves picked (optional)

To make the panna cotta, soak the gelatine leaves in ice cold water (1 cup water per sheet) for 5 minutes to soften.

Put the coconut milk in a medium saucepan over low heat with the sugar, vanilla seeds and lemon zest. Stir until the sugar has dissolved. Add the softened gelatine, stir to combine and remove from the heat. Add the almond milk, and allow the mixture to cool to room temperature.

Fill a small tub with ice and place a large empty bowl in the centre of the ice. Add the yoghurt to the cooled mixture, stir to combine and strain the mixture into the bowl in the ice bath. Stir the mixture until it begins to thicken, which will take 10–25 minutes.

Pour into 10 moulds or glasses. Put in the fridge to set for 12 hours.

Meanwhile, make the honey nut brittle. Preheat the oven to 175°C (345°F) and line a baking tray with baking paper.

Put the honey, almonds, sugar, coconut oil, sea salt and thyme in a medium bowl and mix to combine. Pour the mixture onto the baking tray and spread out.

Bake for 10–15 minutes, or until golden and caramelised.

Allow the brittle to cool then break up and store in an airtight container.

When ready to serve, turn out the panna cotta and scatter over the fresh berries and honey nut brittle.

RAW AVOCADO, CHILLI, CACAO, COCONUT & MACADAMIA TART

Serves 8

Yep, it has avocado and chilli in it, and it's a dessert! Avocado gives this tart the most unreal creamy, silky-smooth texture, almost like a chocolate mousse – not to mention it's considered a superfood. Pow!

4 avocados
1 vanilla bean, split and seeds scraped
150 g (5½ oz) 100 per cent raw cacao powder
5 tablespoons coconut oil
zest of 1 orange
½ red chilli, seeded and diced
4 tablespoons honey
155 g (5½ oz/1 cup) toasted macadamia nuts, chopped

BASE
1 tablespoon chai leaves
160 g (5½ oz/1 cup) pitted dates
80 g (2¾ oz/½ cup) almonds
35 g (1¼ oz/½ cup) shredded coconut
3 tablespoons coconut oil

Brew a cup of chai tea with 250 ml simmering water and chai leaves for 10 minutes.

Put the dates in a small bowl and pour the strained chai tea over them. Set aside to soak overnight.

To make the base, put the soaked dates, almonds, coconut and coconut oil in a food processor and blend until smooth. Press into the base of a 35 cm x 13 cm (14 inch x 5 inch) slice tin. Put in the fridge for 30 minutes to set.

To make the filling, put the avocado flesh in a food processor and give it a buzz. Add the vanilla seeds, cacao powder, coconut oil, zest, chilli and honey and buzz until the mixture comes together.

Spoon on top of the base and scatter over the macadamia nuts. Put in the fridge for at least 2 hours. Slice and serve.

I NEED THIS
NOW!

FRENCH TOAST FINGERS WITH CHOCOLATE HAZELNUT SPREAD & BLUEBERRIES

Serves 6-7

WARNING: This French toast is wickedly indulgent. Enjoy it for breakfast on special occasions, although it's probably better suited to a decadent dessert. Either way, it's freaking tasty!

500 ml (17 fl oz/2 cups) thin (pouring) cream
1 tablespoon honey
15 g (½ oz) butter
zest of 1 orange
1 vanilla bean, split and seeds scraped
4 eggs
150 g (5½ oz) caster (superfine) sugar
1 brioche loaf
2 tablespoons homemade chocolate hazelnut spread
* (see page 228, 'Raw nut butter')*
270 g (9½ oz/1 cup) blueberries
50 ml (1½ fl oz) coconut oil

Preheat oven to 175°C (325°F).

Put the cream, honey, butter, orange zest and vanilla bean in a medium saucepan over medium-high heat. Bring to the boil, stirring, and remove from the heat.

Put the eggs and sugar in a large bowl and whisk to combine.

Pour the hot cream mixture over the egg mixture and whisk to combine.

Using a bread knife, cut the crust off the brioche loaf to create a square log. Slice the loaf in half lengthways. Spread both halves with chocolate hazelnut spread, like you're making a big sandwich, then add the blueberries to the middle and close the sandwich.

Soak the brioche loaf in the warm egg custard for 10 minutes, or until it's well soaked.

Put coconut oil in a medium pan over medium heat and cook the brioche loaf until it's golden brown all over, then finish in the oven for 5 minutes. Transfer to a plate lined with paper towel and slice into fingers.

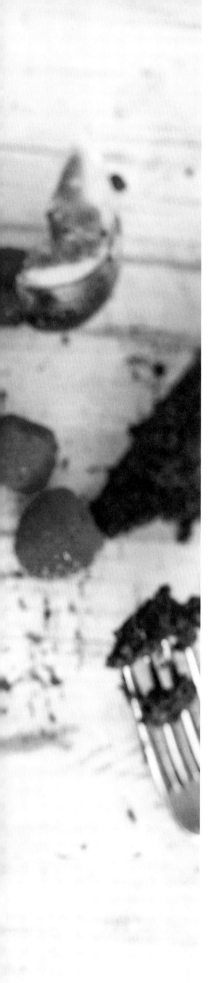

QUINOA MUD CAKE

Yep, you read that correctly − quinoa mud cake. A combination of health food and everyone's favourite decadent treat, it's the ultimate in yin and yang hipster desserts.

> *1 tablespoon coconut oil*
> *65 g (2¼ oz/1 cup) shredded coconut, plus 35 g
>   (1¼ oz/½ cup) extra for dusting the tin*
> *500 g (1 lb 2 oz/2½ cups) cooked quinoa*
> *330 ml (11¼ fl oz/1⅓ cups) coconut water*
> *80 ml (2½ fl oz/⅓ cup) coconut cream*
> *4 eggs*
> *1 teaspoon vanilla extract*
> *zest of 1 orange*
> *185 g (6½ oz/¾ cup) butter*
> *295 g (10¼ oz/1⅓ cup) sugar*
> *105 g (3½ oz/1 cup) 100 per cent raw cacao powder*
> *1½ teaspoons baking powder*
> *⅓ teaspoon bicarbonate of soda (baking soda)*
> *½ teaspoon salt*
> *60 g (2¼ oz/½ cup) raspberries, to serve*
> *2 figs, quartered, to serve*

Preheat the oven to 180°C (350°F).

Brush a 23 cm (9 inch) spring-form cake tin with the coconut oil. Sprinkle the 35 g of shredded coconut over the coconut oil and roll the tin around, so the coconut sticks to the side evenly.

Put the quinoa, coconut water, coconut cream, eggs, vanilla, zest and butter in a food processor and process until smooth. Transfer to a large bowl.

Put the 65 g of shredded coconut, sugar, cacao powder, baking powder, bicarbonate of soda and salt in a medium bowl and mix together.

Add the dry mixture to the quinoa mixture in the large bowl and stir to combine. Pour into the cake tin and bake for 40−60 minutes, or until a skewer inserted into the centre comes out clean.

Serve with the raspberries and figs.

BREAD & BUTTER PUDDING

Serves 8

This is a classic bread & butter pudding recipe with a bit of a Bondi Harvest twist (we love our twists). We've used brioche, which is a sweet and buttery French bread, but you could substitute regular white bread or even croissants if you like. No matter what bread or pastry you choose, it doesn't have to be fresh.

1 litre (35 fl oz/4 cups) full-cream milk
1 vanilla bean, split and seeds scraped
1 cinnamon stick
3 whole cloves
zest of 1 orange
1 brioche loaf
3 eggs
200 g (7 oz) sugar
80 g (2¾ oz/⅓ cup) coconut butter (or regular butter)
110 g (3¾ oz/⅓ cup) jam (we used triple berry)
35 g (1¼ oz/⅓ cup) desiccated coconut, plus extra for dusting
icing sugar, for dusting

Preheat the oven to 200°C (400°F). Grease a large 22 cm x 12 cm (9 inch x 5 inch) loaf tin.

Pour milk into a large saucepan over low heat, and add the vanilla seeds, cinnamon, cloves and orange zest. Heat the milk gently, making sure it does not boil. You want to heat it to about 50°C (120°F), which should take around 5 minutes.

Meanwhile, remove the crusts from the brioche loaf and slice it into three even layers horizontally.

In a medium bowl, lightly whisk the eggs and sugar. Slowly add the warm milk, whisking continuously.

Spread the butter and jam over the bottom two layers of brioche, and sprinkle both layers with coconut. Stack the loaf into the prepared tin, pouring a little of the warm egg custard over each layer before adding the next one. Slowly pour remaining custard over the entire loaf, letting it soak into the brioche between each pour. Dust with extra coconut.

Bake in the oven for 35 minutes, or until golden. Let it cool and set for 30 minutes before turning out onto a board. Dust with icing sugar and slice into pieces to serve.

PEAR, GINGER & THYME TARTE TATIN   *Serves 8*

*One of my all-time favourites, this was the first proper dessert
I learnt to make while doing my apprenticeship. A French
classic I think every foodie should know.*

*6 pears
200 g (7 oz) sugar
zest and juice of 1 lemon
1 cm (½ inch) piece fresh ginger, peeled
50 g (1¾ oz) butter, diced
1 teaspoon fresh thyme leaves, plus extra for garnish
250 g (9 oz) readymade puff pastry
mixed berry, banana, coconut & thyme whip
  (see page 194), to serve*

Preheat the oven to 190°C (375°F).

Peel and core the pears and cut into quarters. Set aside.

Combine the sugar, lemon zest and juice and ginger in a jug and stir to
combine. Pour into a non-stick ovenproof pan or 25 cm (10 inch) tarte
tatin tin over low heat, stirring for 5 minutes, until the sugar is dissolved.
Once the sugar has dissolved, increase the heat to medium and cook for
5 minutes, until the sugar begins to caramelise.

Arrange the pear slices to cover the base of the pan. Dot the pears with
the butter and scatter over the thyme leaves. Cook for 5 minutes, until the
pears are half cooked. Remove the pan from the heat and allow to cool to
room temperature.

Roll out the puff pastry and cut a disc 1 cm (½ inch) larger than the pan.
Place the pastry disc over the caramelised pears, tucking the extra pastry
in underneath the pears.

Cook in the oven for 30–40 minutes, or until the pastry is golden brown.
Remove from the oven and allow to rest for 5 minutes.

Place a plate or large chopping board on top of the pan and invert the
tarte tatin.

Scatter with the remaining thyme and serve warm with the mixed berry,
banana, coconut & thyme whip.

ONE-POT WHITE CHOCOLATE, COCONUT & MACADAMIA CAKE

Serves 8

Let's not make baking difficult – if you've got a non-stick pot or spring-form tray, smash it all together and let the oven do all the hard work. This recipe is one that's good for the soul rather than the belly! We've garnished the cake with honeycomb and cacao nibs here, but you could also crush up half a Crunchie or Violet Crumble bar instead.

250 g (9 oz) butter, coarsely chopped
450 g (1 lb) white chocolate, coarsely chopped
350 g (12 oz/1⅔ cups) sugar
250 ml (9 fl oz/1 cup) coconut cream
340 g (11¾ oz/2⅓ cups) self-raising flour
1 teaspoon vanilla extract
2 eggs, whisked
zest of 1 lemon
60 g (2¼ oz/½ cup) chopped macadamia nuts
35 g (1¼ oz/½ cup) shredded coconut
30 g (1 oz/½ cup) crushed honeycomb
45 g (1½ oz/¼ cup) cacao nibs
60 g (2¼ oz/½ cup) dried cranberries

Preheat the oven to 160°C (320°F).

Put a 23 cm (9 inch) ovenproof saucepan over low heat. Add the butter, chocolate, sugar and coconut cream and cook, stirring, until the mixture is smooth, without boiling.

Sift the flour into the saucepan and add the vanilla, egg, lemon zest and macadamias and mix until a smooth batter. Sprinkle over the coconut.

Put the saucepan in the oven and cook for 1 hour, then cover the top and sides with foil and bake for a further 45 minutes.

Rest the cake for 30 minutes before turning out, or just serve it in the pan. Sprinkle over the honeycomb, cacao nibs and cranberries before serving.

BASICS

This chapter is probably the most important part of this book, we reckon, because learning these basic recipes will give you more control over what you eat.

How often do you go to the supermarket and check the ingredients list on the back of a packet, only to find a bunch of additives you've never heard of hiding in the food you want to buy? But unlocking just how simple it is to create your own butters, milks and breads means you can rely less on store-bought processed products and instead know exactly what's in your food.

Knowing how to make the basics also minimises waste in the kitchen, which is just as important as sourcing local produce and eating seasonally.

This chapter is full of recipes and tips for turning your leftovers into something new and turning your kitchen into a whole-food one. It's all about having a much more balanced approach to cooking, eating and food.

WHAT OILS TO USE

Not all oils are created equal. In fact, despite what has been common belief, some oils actually provide health benefits.

The healthiest oils and fats are the polyunsaturated ones, which include grapeseed and walnut oils. They contain omega-6 and omega-3, which lower the 'bad' LDL cholesterol and increase the 'good' HDL cholesterol. Monounsaturated fats are also good as they can help boost good cholesterol.

Grapeseed Oil

High in polyunsaturated fats and vitamin E, this oil is one you can feel good about using. Grapeseed oil has a high smoke point, which makes it perfect for stir-frying and sautéing, and it's practically flavourless so your ingredients can be the star of the show.

Walnut Oil

Unlike grapeseed oil, this has a low smoke point, so it doesn't perform well under heat, but its nutty flavour lends itself perfectly to salad dressings. It contains polyunsaturated fats, including alpha-linoleic acid (a heart-healthy, anti-inflammatory omega-3) and vitamin K, which can strengthen bones.

Avocado Oil

Avocado oil is high in monounsaturated fat, and lends a lovely flavour to vinaigrettes or drizzled over fish. Like other specialty oils, it can be on the pricey side, so refrigerate it to keep its subtle avocado flavour fresh, and bring it to room temperature before using.

ACTIVATED NUTS Makes 2 cups

Simply put, activated nuts are nuts that have been soaked in water for a period of time, to activate the germination process. The nuts are then dehydrated at a low temperature.

Why activate nuts? Well, activating them increases their nutrient value and helps with digestion. Nuts are full of great minerals like zinc, calcium and magnesium, as well as proteins and healthy fats, but raw nuts have enzymes and phytic acid that inhibits absorption of all these goodies. Activating nuts fixes these issues.

300 g (10½ oz/2 cups) nuts

Place nuts, 4 cups of water and a pinch of salt in a container and let them soak for at least 10 hours.

Preheat the oven or dehydrator to 85°C (185°F).

Strain the nuts, place them on a baking tray and leave in the oven for at least 15 hours. Make sure they are completely dehydrated, otherwise they will go mouldy.

Store in an airtight container for up to 2 weeks, and eat, or use to make nut milk and butters.

SPROUTING SEEDS Makes 1 cup

Sprouts are epic in raw salads and are great in tasty green smoothies and soups.

140 g (5 oz/1 cup) seeds or beans

Place the seeds or beans into a large mason jar, and fill the rest of the jar with warm filtered water and a pinch of sea salt. Cut a piece of cheesecloth or breathable mesh to size, and secure the cloth over the top of the jar with the band, but not the lid. You could also use a rubber band to secure the cloth. Leave to soak for at least 12 hours.

Without removing the cloth, rinse the seeds or beans by straining out the soaking water, then filling the jar with fresh water and giving it a shake. Strain out the fresh water then turn the jar upside down and place in a sunny spot at an angle so that air can circulate, and the water can drain off.

Repeat this process at least twice daily.

In 1 to 4 days, the sprouts will be ready. Rinse sprouts well, drain, and store in the jar (with the lid replaced) in the fridge.

Eat within 2 to 3 days.

COCONUT BUTTER Makes 1 cup

This recipe only requires two ingredients: desiccated coconut, and a lot of patience. At first it will seem like the desiccated coconut will never turn into butter, but once the oil from the coconut starts to get released, you'll get a smooth, velvety coconut butter as if by magic. Trust us, it's worth the wait.

180–270 g (6–9½ oz/2–3 cups) desiccated coconut

Put the desiccated coconut in a high-speed blender and blend until it starts to form a smooth paste. This can take up to 15 minutes. Store in an airtight container in the fridge.

COW'S BUTTER AND BUTTERMILK

Makes 1 cup butter and 1 cup buttermilk

Butter has received a bit of a bad wrap in the past, but good-quality unprocessed butter actually contains beneficial saturated fat, so it's a far better alternative to processed spreads like margarine. When you make it yourself, you know exactly what's in it and what processes it went through to end up in your fridge. What's better than that?

500 ml (17 fl oz/2 cups) thin (pouring) cream

Put the cream in an electric mixer and, using the whisk attachment, mix for 10 minutes. The cream will thicken, then change colour to start to look like butter. Keep the mixer going past this point until suddenly the buttermilk drops out.

Using a strainer, strain the buttermilk into a separate bowl, then use your hands to squeeze out any leftover liquid from the butter. To finish, put the butter into ice water to wash off any leftover buttermilk. Store the butter and buttermilk in airtight containers in the fridge.

If you want to infuse other flavours into the butter, such as thyme, truffle oil or garlic, simply add these at the beginning of the mixing process.

COLD-PRESSED VIRGIN COCONUT OIL

Makes 1 cup

Before long, you'll be using this on everything – I know I do!

5 coconuts
5 cups water

Crack open the coconuts, remove the liquid (put it in the fridge to use later), and scrape out the coconut flesh using a spoon.

In batches, put the coconut flesh in a blender with the water and blend for 10 minutes, or until smooth. Transfer the mixture to a large bowl and using your hands, work and squeeze the pulp for about 20 minutes.

Strain the mixture into a large bowl lined with cheesecloth and squeeze out the liquid, reserving it in a jug. Repeat the straining and squeezing process 3 times, reserving all of the liquid (the pulp can be dehydrated and made into flour).

Pour the liquid into a jar with a large opening, cover with plastic wrap and set aside at room temperature for at least 48 hours.

Transfer to the fridge and refrigerate for 1 hour to help solidify the oil.

The solid layer on top is the oil; carefully scrape off this solid layer and store in an airtight container in the fridge until needed.

HOMEMADE TAHINI

Makes 1/3 cup

Used in our stuffed capsicum dressing, homemade tahini's also epic just on toast with honey and banana.

145 g (5 oz/1 cup) sesame seeds, toasted
1½ tablespoons sesame oil

Put the sesame seeds in a food processor and process for 20–30 minutes, stopping and scraping down the side as needed every 5 minutes.

Add the sesame oil and salt to taste, if you like, and process until a smooth paste forms.

Transfer to a glass jar, seal and store in the fridge.

RAW NUT BUTTER

Makes 1-2 cups

Don't like dairy butter? Give this a try. You can use almost any nut, so get creative.

2–3 cups nuts of your choice, such as peanuts, hazelnuts, almonds, pistachios or cashews
1 teaspoon raw cacao (optional)

Put the nuts in a food processor and process for 20–30 minutes, stopping and scraping down the side as needed every 5 minutes. This takes more time than you'd expect, so be patient! It's ready when the oils have released from the nuts and the consistency is like smooth butter.

Stir in the raw cacao to make a delicious chocolate spread.

Transfer to a glass jar, seal and store in the fridge.

CULTURED BUTTER AND BUTTERMILK

Makes 1 cup butter and 1 cup buttermilk

This butter has a zingy flavour and is good for your belly.

500 ml (17 fl oz/2 cups) thin (pouring) cream
2 tablespoons cultured yoghurt

Start by making cultured cream. Put the cream in a small saucepan over medium heat and bring to the culturing temperature of 37.5°C (99.5°F). Remove the saucepan from the heat, add the cultured yoghurt and mix well.

If the saucepan has a tight-fitting lid, put that on. If not, transfer the mixture to a jar and screw the lid tight. Wrap the saucepan or jar in a warm towel or blanket and put in the warmest part of the house. Leave it there for 15–20 hours.

Transfer the saucepan or jar to the fridge to chill.

Put the cream in an electric mixer and, using the whisk attachment, mix for 10 minutes, or until the cream thickens, changes colour and starts to look like butter. Keep the mixer going past this point until suddenly the buttermilk drops out.

Using a strainer, strain the buttermilk off into a separate bowl, then use your hands to squeeze out any excess liquid. Place your butter into ice water to wash off any leftover buttermilk. Store the butter and buttermilk in airtight containers in the fridge.

CHAI NUT MILK

 Makes 1 litre (35 fl oz)

A must for all smoothie enthusiasts.

1½ cups raw nuts of choice, such as almonds, macadamias or pistachios
1 litre (35 fl oz/4 cups) hot water
1½ teaspoons chai leaves
1 vanilla bean, split and seeds scraped

Soak the nuts in water overnight. Strain and discard the water.

Brew chai tea with hot water, chai leaves and vanilla, and let it steep for 5 minutes. Then strain the hot tea into a blender, and add the nuts.

Pulse to break up the nuts, then blend until all ingredients are liquid.

Strain through muslin or cheesecloth. Bottle and store in the fridge for up to 3 days.

HONEY VANILLA RICE MILK

 Makes 1 litre (35 fl oz)

Make it at home so you know exactly what's gone in it – all the right goodies for all the right reasons.

2 cups cooked brown or white rice, or cooked quinoa
1.5 litres (52 fl oz/6 cups) water
1 tablespoon honey
1 vanilla bean, split and seeds scraped

Put the rice or quinoa in a blender with the water, honey and vanilla seeds.

Pulse to break up the rice or quinoa, and then blend until all ingredients are liquid.

Strain through muslin or cheesecloth. Bottle and store in the fridge for up to 3 days.

COCONUT MILK

 Makes 1-2 cups

Fresh is best – it's time to make curries from scratch with your own coconut milk.

5 coconuts

Crack open the coconuts and reserve the liquid. Scrape out all the coconut flesh using a spoon.

Put the coconut flesh and the reserved coconut water in a blender and blend until smooth . . . that's it.

Strain through muslin or cheesecloth if you don't like the consistency.

PASTRAMI MEAT RUB

  Makes 1 cup

Make this up and store it in your pantry and, I'm telling you, your barbecues will never smell the same again.

1 tablespoon garlic powder
1 tablespoon ground coriander
3 tablespoons smoked paprika
1 tablespoon dark brown sugar
5 tablespoons black peppercorns, toasted
4 tablespoons sea salt

Put all the ingredients in a mortar and break up using the pestle. Pound and grind for 5 minutes, or until a coarse consistency. Store in an airtight container.

INFUSED SALTS

Infused salts are a great and easy way to add attitude to your cooking, curing and seasoning.

GRAVLAX SALT RUB

Makes 2 cups

Rub this over a salmon fillet, let it sit in the fridge overnight and BAM – gravlax salmon done.

1 tablespoon black peppercorns, toasted
220 g (7¾ oz/1 cup) sugar
290 g (10¼ oz/1 cup) salt
2 tablespoons fennel seeds, toasted
zest of 2 lemons
zest of 1 orange
zest of 1 lime

Put the black peppercorns in the bowl of a mortar and break up well using the pestle. Add the other ingredients and grind gently to mix. Store in airtight container.

BONDI HARVEST BASIC SALT RUB

Makes 2 cups

580 g (20½ oz/2 cups) salt
2 sprigs thyme
2 sprigs rosemary
2 bay leaves
4 tablespoons black pepper
4 tablespoons fennel seeds

Combine all ingredients in a medium bowl and store in an airtight container.

CITRUS SALT

Makes 1 cup

290 g (10¼ oz/1 cup) salt
zest of 1 lemon
zest of 1 lime
zest of 1 orange

Combine all ingredients in a medium bowl and store in an airtight container.

CHILLI PEPPER SALT

Makes 1 cup

½ tablespoon black peppercorns, toasted
4 red chillies, halved, seeded
290 g (10¼ oz/1 cup) salt

Break up the peppercorns using a mortar and pestle. Put the chillies and salt in a bowl, add the peppercorns and mix well. Store in an airtight container.

CELERY SALT

Makes 1 cup

50 g (1¾ oz/1 cup) celery leaves
290 g (10¼ oz/1 cup) salt
zest of 1 lemon

Preheat the oven to 175°C (345°F). Line a baking tray with baking paper and spread the celery leaves over it. Dehydrate the leaves in the oven for 5 minutes, or until crisp but not burnt.

Mix the dried leaves with the salt and lemon zest. Store in an airtight container.

SAUCES AND CONDIMENTS

AÏOLI

Makes 1 litre

You can do it with a machine or whisk it by hand, but you've got to know how to make a great aïoli. It's an absolute everyday essential.

1 head of garlic
1 litre (35 fl oz/4 cups) olive oil, plus extra
   for roasting garlic
3 eggs
3 egg yolks, extra
1 tablespoon dijon mustard
1 tablespoon white wine vinegar

To roast the garlic, preheat the oven to 180°C (350°F). Toss the garlic in olive oil, put on a baking tray lined with baking paper and cook for 15–20 minutes, until soft. Allow to cool, then squeeze the garlic flesh into a small bowl.

Method 1: Put the eggs, extra egg yolks, mustard, vinegar and 1 tablespoon of the roasted garlic in a food processor or blender. Start the motor, then slowly drizzle in the oil. Season with salt and pepper to taste.

Method 2: Put the eggs, extra egg yolks, mustard, vinegar and 1 tablespoon of the roasted garlic in a large bowl. Combine using a whisk, then start drizzling in the oil very slowly, whisking continuously, until the aïoli is thick and creamy. Season with salt and pepper to taste.

YOGHURT TARTAR

 Makes 600 ml (21 fl oz)

Using yoghurt instead of oils to make tartar sauce does three things: it lowers the fat content; gives it a zingy yoghurt tang; and also brings probiotic cultures into your diet. It's a win, win, win.

1 small handful parsley, leaves coarsely chopped
1 small handful coriander (cilantro), leaves
   coarsely chopped
250 g (9 oz) gherkins (pickles), coarsely chopped
1 tablespoon capers, drained and coarsely chopped
260 g (9¼ oz/1 cup) Greek-style yoghurt
1 tablespoon dijon mustard
juice of 1 lemon

Put all of the ingredients in a large jar and mix well. Season with salt and pepper and store in the fridge in an airtight container.

SMOKY CHILLI JAM

  Makes 2 cups

This takes a bit of time, but it's well worth the effort. Once you've tried this, you'll turn up your nose to any other chilli sauce that comes your way.

250 ml (9 fl oz/1 cup) coconut oil
1 onion, diced
4 garlic cloves, minced
1 teaspoon smoked paprika
1 cm (½ inch) piece fresh ginger, chopped
1½ red capsicums (peppers), charred, skin
   removed and diced
3 red chillies, charred, skin removed and diced
   (keep the seeds)
175 g (6 oz) tinned tomatoes
175 g (6 oz) palm sugar (jaggery)
200 ml (7 fl oz) fish or chicken stock
   (see page 236 or 238)

Heat coconut oil in a large saucepan or stockpot over medium heat. Add the onion, garlic, paprika, ginger, capsicum, chilli, tomato and palm sugar and cook for about 10–15 minutes, or until caramelised and collapsed. Add the stock and cook for 10 minutes. Set aside to cool.

Purée the mixture in a blender in batches. Store the jam in an airtight 500 ml (17 fl oz/2 cup) container.

SALSA VERDE

  Makes 1 cup

Salsa verde literally means 'green sauce'. It's zesty and herbaceous and goes perfectly with any seafood.

1 spring onion (scallion), diced
½ cup chopped parsley
½ cup chopped mint
½ cup chopped basil
½ tablespoon dijon mustard
½ tablespoon capers, drained and finely chopped
100 ml (3½ fl oz) extra virgin olive oil
3 anchovies, diced
1 garlic clove, minced

Combine all ingredients in a medium bowl. Season with salt and pepper to taste and store in an airtight container in the fridge.

KALE PESTO

 Makes 1 x 300 ml (10½ fl oz) jar

This is definitely not a traditional pesto, but it's just as tasty. The addition of kale not only ups the hipster level but the health benefits too, and the almonds add flavour and oils.

1 garlic clove
200 ml (7 fl oz) olive oil
3 pinches of sea salt flakes
½ cup picked basil leaves
½ cup finely chopped kale leaves
½ cup toasted almonds
zest and juice of ½ lemon
½ cup finely grated parmesan cheese

We like to use a mortar and pestle to make our pesto. Put the garlic with a little of the olive oil and a pinch of sea salt in the mortar (bowl). Push with the pestle to break up the garlic until you have a paste.

Add the basil, a little more olive oil and a pinch of sea salt. Grind the basil with the pestle to break it down to a paste. Repeat with the kale.

Add the almonds and break up a little with the pestle.

Add the lemon zest and juice, and the parmesan cheese and pound with the pestle to get a pesto consistency.

Store in an airtight container in the fridge.

HOLLANDAISE Serves 2-3

Want to really impress someone with breakfast in bed? Then this is a must. Once you've mastered this basic recipe, feel free to make it your own and try some different flavours.

3 egg yolks
2 tablespoons apple cider vinegar
juice of 1 lemon
175 g (6 oz) 'grass-fed' butter, diced

Half-fill a medium saucepan with water and bring to a simmer over medium heat.

Put the egg yolks, vinegar and lemon juice in a heatproof bowl that will fit over the saucepan.

Place the bowl over the simmering saucepan to create a double-boiler and, using a whisk, whisk the mixture continuously for 5 minutes, until light ribbons begin to form. Add the butter one cube at a time, whisking to incorporate each one, and keeping the water at a light simmer.

Once all the butter is incorporated, season with salt and pepper and serve immediately.

BASIC TOMATO SAUCE

Makes 2-3 cups

Or sugo, the way Nonna used to make it.

60 ml (2 fl oz/¼ cup) olive oil
4 garlic cloves, minced
1 red chilli, minced (keep the seeds if you like it hot)
3 onions, diced
500 g (1 lb 2 oz) tinned diced tomatoes
1 tablespoon fresh oregano leaves

Heat the olive oil in a large heavy-based saucepan over medium heat. Add the garlic, chilli and onion and cook until the onion is tender. Add the tomato, reduce the heat to low and cook for 1 hour. Season with salt and pepper to taste. Remove from the heat.

Put the sauce in a blender and blend in batches. Stir through the oregano and serve with pasta or use as a base for other recipes.

GUACAMOLE Serves 4

Everyone's super Mexican friend. Served with tacos or just some corn chips, there's always space for guac on my table.

1 avocado
1 large handful coriander (cilantro), leaves chopped
juice of 1 lime
juice of 1 lemon
½ garlic clove, minced

Put all ingredients in a medium bowl and mash like it's a mosh pit. Season with salt and pepper and dig in.

STOCKS

FISH STOCK

Makes about 3 litres
(105 fl oz/12 cups)

I catch a lot of fish and, out of respect, I make sure I use the whole fish, including the bones. Fish stock is a great way to use the bones.

2 kg (4 lb 8 oz) fish bones, chopped
50 ml (1½ fl oz/2½ tablespoons) olive oil
1 garlic clove, chopped
1 onion, sliced
1 leek, white part only, sliced
2 celery sticks, sliced
½ fennel bulb, sliced
250 ml (9 fl oz/1 cup) white wine
4 bay leaves
1 sprig thyme
1 sprig rosemary
6 parsley stalks

Clean the fish bones with running water, washing away any blood and discarding all innards.

Heat the oil in a stockpot or large saucepan over medium heat. Add the garlic, onion, leek, celery and fennel and sweat for 10 minutes, or until the vegetables are soft but not coloured. Add the fish bones and cook for 5 minutes. Add the wine and cook for 5 minutes, or until reduced by half.

Add 4 litres (135 fl oz/16 cups) water, bay leaves, thyme, rosemary and parsley stalks and simmer for 20–30 minutes. Don't allow the stock to boil or it will become cloudy.

Strain through a fine strainer or muslin. Allow to cool and store in an airtight container in the fridge for up to 3 days or in the freezer for up to 3 months.

CHICKEN STOCK Makes about 3 litres (105 fl oz/12 cups)

Chicken stock's my go-to stock for risottos, as it's full-flavoured without being overpowering.

2 chicken carcasses
1 onion, chopped
2 garlic cloves, chopped
2 red chillies, chopped (keep the seeds)
4 celery sticks, chopped
2 carrots, chopped
3 bay leaves
2 sprigs rosemary
4 black peppercorns

Place all the ingredients in a large saucepan with 8 litres (270 fl oz/32 cups) water over high heat. Bring to the boil, reduce the heat to a simmer and cook for 2–4 hours.

Ladle the fat from the surface of the stock. Strain through a fine strainer or muslin. Allow to cool to room temperature and refrigerate in an airtight container for up to 5 days or freeze for up to 4 months.

BEEF STOCK Makes about 3 litres (105 fl oz/12 cups)

Or, if you're hipster, bone broth. Beef stock/bone broth is ridiculously good for you and super cheap. Make a big batch and freeze it, and you'll always be ready for a cold rainy night.

2 kg (4 lb 8 oz) beef bones, chopped into
   5 cm (2 inch) pieces
150 ml (5 fl oz) olive oil
2 onions, chopped
1 head of garlic, halved
2 carrots, chopped
2 celery sticks, chopped
90 g (3¼ oz/1 cup) chopped mushrooms
6 parsley stalks
4 black peppercorns
2 sprigs thyme
2 sprigs rosemary
4 bay leaves

Preheat the oven to 180°C (350°F). Put the beef bones in a large roasting tray and roast for 5–8 minutes, until golden.

Meanwhile, heat the olive oil in a stockpot or large saucepan over medium-high heat. Add the onion, garlic, carrot, celery and mushroom and cook until tender and slightly coloured.

Add the roasted bones, parsley stalks, black peppercorns, thyme, rosemary, bay leaves and 8 litres (270 fl oz/32 cups) water and increase the heat to high. Bring to the boil (this should take about 10 minutes), skimming the fats and impurities the whole time, then reduce the heat to a light simmer and cook for 4 hours, skimming the surface every 30 minutes.

Strain the stock through a fine strainer or muslin. Allow to cool and store in an airtight container in the fridge for up to 3 days or in the freezer for up to 3 months.

SHELLFISH BROTH Makes about 3 litres (105 fl oz/12 cups)

'Never waste anything' is what you get taught in a professional kitchen. Just freeze your prawn shells and fish skeletons and, when you have enough, pull them out and boom – shellfish broth city.

2 kg (4 lb 8 oz) fish bones and heads, chopped,
   and shellfish shells
50 ml (1½ fl oz/2½ tablespoons) olive oil
1 garlic clove, chopped
1 onion, sliced
1 leek, white part only, sliced
2 celery sticks, sliced
½ fennel bulb, sliced
1 tablespoon tomato paste (concentrated purée)
3 tomatoes, diced
250 ml (9 fl oz/1 cup) white wine
pinch of saffron
4 bay leaves
1 sprig thyme
1 sprig rosemary
6 parsley stalks

Clean the fish bones and shellfish shells with running water, washing away any blood and discarding all innards.

Heat the oil in a stock pot or large saucepan over medium heat. Add the garlic, onion, leek, celery and fennel and sweat for 10 minutes, or until the vegetables are soft but not coloured. Add the fish bones and shellfish shells and cook for 5 minutes. Add the tomato paste, tomato, wine and saffron and cook for 5 minutes, or until reduced by half.

Add 4 litres (135 fl oz/16 cups) water, bay leaves, thyme, rosemary and parsley stalks, and simmer for 20–30 minutes. Don't allow the stock to boil or it will become cloudy.

Strain through a fine strainer or muslin. Allow to cool and store in an airtight container in the fridge for up to 3 days or in the freezer for up to 3 months.

VEGETABLE STOCK  Makes about 3 litres (105 fl oz/12 cups)

This stock is so simple and adds loads of flavour and extra nutrients when cooking quinoa and grains.

1 head of garlic, halved
500 g (1 lb 2 oz) mushrooms, chopped
3 celery sticks, chopped
3 onions, chopped
3 carrots, chopped
7 parsley stalks
4 black peppercorns
3 sprigs thyme
2 sprigs rosemary
4 bay leaves

Put all the ingredients in a stockpot or large saucepan with 8 litres (270 fl oz/32 cups) over medium heat. Cook for 2–3 hours at a simmer.

Strain the stock through a fine strainer or muslin cloth. Allow to cool and store in an airtight container in the fridge for up to 3 days or freeze for up to 3 months.

GRAINS AND SEEDS

BONDI HARVEST GRANOLA Serves 5

This recipe is a mosh pit of everything good for you and it's so simple to make. I've always got granola handy in my pantry for a quick breakfast or a late-night guilt-free snack.

40 g (1½ oz/⅓ cup) rice bran (available from health or natural food stores)
30 g (1 oz/1 cup) puffed rice
100 g (3½ oz/¾ cup) sunflower seeds
225 g (8 oz/1¼ cup) roasted buckwheat (available from health or natural food stores)
75 g (2½ oz/⅓ cup) rolled amaranth (available from health or natural food stores)
30 g (1 oz/1 cup) puffed millet (available from health or natural food stores)
60 g (2 oz/½ cup) dried cranberries
90 g (3 oz/¾ cup) sultanas
90 g (3 oz/¾ cup) currants
40 g (1½ oz/¼ cup) goji berries
80 g (2¾ oz/½ cup) almonds
60 g (2 oz/¼ cup) banana chips
80 g (2¾ oz/⅔ cup) pepitas (pumpkin seeds)

Mix all the ingredients together in a bowl and transfer to an airtight container. Store in a cool dry place for up to 3 weeks.

HOW TO COOK MILLET  Makes 3 cups

Millet is a little like couscous, but it has the most epic nutty flavour and it's gluten-free.

210 g (7½ oz/1 cup) millet
1 tablespoon coconut oil
500 ml (17 fl oz/2 cups) water or stock
1 whole garlic clove (optional)
1 red chilli, sliced in half (optional)
1 cinnamon stick (optional)

Run the millet under water for 5 minutes and drain in a fine mesh sieve.

Heat coconut oil in a medium saucepan over medium heat. Add the millet and toast until dry and golden (but not burnt) with a nutty taste and fragrance.

Add the water or stock and garlic, chilli and cinnamon, if using, stir and bring to the boil. Reduce the heat to low and cook for 15 minutes, or until the liquid is absorbed.

Remove the saucepan from the heat and set aside for 10 minutes to finish cooking.

Remove the garlic, chilli and cinnamon, fluff the millet with a fork and serve.

HOW TO COOK QUINOA Makes 3 cups

The most popular of superfoods, this is a must for any home cook's arsenal, and it's so simple.

190 g (6½ oz/1 cup) uncooked quinoa
500 ml (17 fl oz/2 cups) water or stock
1 sprig thyme, leaves picked (optional)
1 whole garlic clove (optional)

Rinse the quinoa under water in a strainer for 5 minutes.

Heat the water or stock in a medium saucepan over medium heat. Add the quinoa, thyme and garlic, if using. Cover and bring to the boil. Turn heat to low and cook for 15 minutes, or until the quinoa becomes translucent. Remove the garlic before serving.

ACKNOWLEDGEMENTS

Mark: This book is the latest high in the amazing ride that has been Bondi Harvest. There's a ridiculously large number of people I'd like to thank for making the ride possible, but here goes:

Firstly, huge thanks to my partner in all things Bondi Harvest, Guy Turland. I'm grateful to not only work alongside you and to share our incredible food philosophy, but to be able to call you a mate.

Bondi Harvest has always been about good food and good times – so I'd like to give special thanks to Rebecca Bernstone for introducing me to good food (I can now say that your pesto literally changed my life); and to John Kettle, Hayes Montgomery, Trent Young and Scott Stanners for (if not introducing me to, then at least perfecting the art of) good times.

Thanks also to HarperCollins and Catherine Milne for the leap of faith in publishing our book, as well as patience, guidance and good vibes along the way.

Thanks to my family – Mum and Dad, Shirl and Pete, and my sisters, Louise, Megan and Catherine. Your support has been invaluable, and all the awesome beetroot risotto in the world will never be able to pay that back.

To Eddie and Sunny – you two will never know the depth of love and joy you bring to my life.

Finally, and most enormously of all – thanks, admiration and love forever to my wife, Loosie Craig. Your ideas, support, understanding, insights and love are what have brought me here. Everything I've put between these pages is thanks to you.

*

Guy: BH is a two-man team, so the first thanks go the big fella behind the camera and in control of all the production: the beard, Mark Alston! You're a legend and it's been a pleasure building the beast that is Bondi Harvest with you.

I've been working in professional kitchens from the age of 16 and wanted to say a massive YEW to all the chefs, waiters and now friends that have been a part of that journey. This book comes from an honest place and is an incorporation of all the knowledge and lessons I've learnt from you.

I dedicate this book to my family. I'm so lucky to have such an epic family; without their understanding, love and support over the last two and a half years, none of what we have achieved would have been possible. Knowing I have your support makes every battle, decision and 12-hour day seem easy.

*

We would both also like to thank Stephen Baccon, Dean Bates, Jake Harris, Jordy Levin, Mark Bocci, Steve Kydd, Lisa Goldstone, Tastemade, Rachel Krupa, Ros Bellenger, David Malina, David Jansen, Tom Philips, Infinity2, Renee Lord, Charlie Boyce, Brittany Bennett, Tara Madden, Sarah Montgomery, Chris Young and Caz Morley, the Depot team, and Vicky Dragaud Matovanni.

ABOUT THE AUTHORS

Mark Alston

A farm boy from outside Wagga Wagga, Mark came to Sydney to pursue a career in film-making – and he got one! Mark found himself working on back-to-back feature films, including The Matrix Reloaded and The Matrix Revolutions, Star Wars Episode III, The Last Samurai, The Chronicles of Narnia, Ghost Rider, Stealth and Man of Steel, a personal dream come true.

Mark began his directing career with two short films that screened in over 35 countries and won multiple awards. He then turned his attention to directing acclaimed music videos for artists such as the John Butler Trio, Jessica Mauboy, Guy Sebastian, and Kate Miller-Heidke, for which he was nominated for an ARIA in the Best Music Video category.

Mark has also directed commercials and online films for top international brands including Louis Vuitton, Asics, Volvo, Westfield and Breville, amongst others. Now, Mark has altered his course again to reconnect to food and produce as a co-creator of Bondi Harvest.

Guy Turland

Originally from Bowral, Guy moved to Bondi in 2003 for his chef's apprenticeship. Upon finishing, he was snapped up by some of Sydney's top kitchens, including est., which won Restaurant of the Year in Guy's first year there.

A common love for surfing and food saw executive head chef of est. Peter Doyle become Guy's personal mentor, and, under his guidance, Guy learnt all aspects of the kitchen. As Guy puts it, 'Every chef has a career-defining experience, and this was mine.'

In 2007, Guy moved on to Bondi Icebergs, attracted by chef Rob Marchetti's simple and respectful approach to Italian cooking. He spent two years fine-tuning his skills there, and left in 2009 in pursuit of his dream of starting his own establishment. In March of the same year he bought a run-down café in North Bondi, now called Jo and Willy's Depot, where Guy has creative control of the kitchen.

A keen free diver, Guy and his mates dive most weeks and know where and when the fish are running in Bondi's fertile waters. Always mindful about catching sustainably, the boys are often seen carrying lobsters or kingfish as big as your arm home for a cook-up with friends.

INDEX

HarperCollins*Publishers*

First published in Australia in 2015
by HarperCollins*Publishers* Australia Pty Limited
ABN 36 009 913 517
harpercollins.com.au

Text copyright © Bondi Harvest Pty Ltd 2015
Photography copyright © Stephen Baccon 2015

HarperCollins*Publishers*
Level 13, 201 Elizabeth Street, Sydney NSW 2000, Australia
Unit D1, 63 Apollo Drive, Rosedale, Auckland 0632, New Zealand
A 53, Sector 57, Noida, UP, India
1 London Bridge Street, London SE1 9GF, United Kingdom
2 Bloor Street East, 20th floor, Toronto, Ontario M4W 1A8, Canada
195 Broadway, New York, NY 10007, USA

National Library of Australia Cataloguing-in-Publication data:

Turland, Guy, author.
  Bondi harvest / Guy Turland and Mark Alston; Stephen Baccon (photographer).
  978 0 7322 9986 6 (paperback)
  Includes index.
  Cooking, Australian.
  Cooking – New South Wales – Bondi.
  Other Creators/Contributors: Alston, Mark, author.
  Baccon, Stephen, photographer.
641.5994

Cover and internal photography by Stephen Baccon
Styling by Bondi Harvest
Internal illustrations by Daniel Giscard Hernandez
Photograph on page 12 © Jason Corroto
Props courtesy of Prop Stop and Major & Toms
With thanks to the Bondi Harvest community and the team at Depot
  for taking part in the photographic stories
Cover and internal design by Matt Stanton, HarperCollins Design Studio
Internal layout by Jane Waterhouse
Colour reproduction by Graphic Print Group, Adelaide
Printed and bound in China by RR Donnelley

5 4 3 2 1   15 16 17 18